Samuel French Acting Edition

The Knack

A Comedy in Three Acts

by Ann Jellicoe

SAMUELFRENCH.COM   SAMUELFRENCH.CO.UK

Copyright © 1958, 1962 by Ann Jellicoe
All Rights Reserved

THE KNACK is fully protected under the copyright laws of the United States of America, the British Commonwealth, including Canada, and all other countries of the Copyright Union. All rights, including professional and amateur stage productions, recitation, lecturing, public reading, motion picture, radio broadcasting, television and the rights of translation into foreign languages are strictly reserved.

ISBN 978-0-573-61125-4

www.SamuelFrench.com
www.SamuelFrench.co.uk

FOR PRODUCTION ENQUIRIES

UNITED STATES AND CANADA
Info@SamuelFrench.com
1-866-598-8449

UNITED KINGDOM AND EUROPE
Plays@SamuelFrench.co.uk
020-7255-4302

Each title is subject to availability from Samuel French, depending upon country of performance. Please be aware that *THE KNACK* may not be licensed by Samuel French in your territory. Professional and amateur producers should contact the nearest Samuel French office or licensing partner to verify availability.

CAUTION: Professional and amateur producers are hereby warned that *THE KNACK* is subject to a licensing fee. Publication of this play(s) does not imply availability for performance. Both amateurs and professionals considering a production are strongly advised to apply to Samuel French before starting rehearsals, advertising, or booking a theatre. A licensing fee must be paid whether the title(s) is presented for charity or gain and whether or not admission is charged. Professional/Stock licensing fees are quoted upon application to Samuel French.

No one shall make any changes in this title(s) for the purpose of production. No part of this book may be reproduced, stored in a retrieval system, or transmitted in any form, by any means, now known or yet to be invented, including mechanical, electronic, photocopying, recording, videotaping, or otherwise, without the prior written permission of the publisher. No one shall upload this title(s), or part of this title(s), to any social media websites.

For all enquiries regarding motion picture, television, and other media rights, please contact Samuel French.

Please refer to page 95 for further copyright information.

THE KNACK, by Ann Jellicoe, directed by Mike Nichols, was produced by The Establishment Theatre Co., Inc., by arrangement with David Black, at The New Theatre, N. Y. C.

CAST
(In Order of Appearance)

TOM	*Brian Bedford*
COLIN	*Roddy Maude-Roxby*
TOLEN	*Brian Murray*
NANCY	*Alexandra Berlin*

SCENES

The play, in three acts, takes place in a room in London.

DESCRIPTION OF CHARACTERS

TOM: Smallish in size. Vigorous, balanced, strong and sensitive in his movements. He speaks with a great range of pitch, pace and volume and with immense energy and vitality.

COLIN: Tall and uncoordinated. Explodes into speech and talks jerkily, flatly, haltingly. Basically a strong and intelligent man, but unsure of himself. Gets very angry with himself.

TOLEN: Once an unpromising physical specimen he has developed himself by systematic physical exercise. His body is now much as he would like it to be. He appears strong, well-built, full of rippling muscle. All his movements are a conscious display of this body. He almost always speaks with a level, clipped smoothness and a very considered subtlety of tone.

NANCY: Aged about seventeen. Potentially a beautiful girl but her personality, like her appearance, is still blurred and unformed. She wears an accordion-pleated skirt.

The Knack

ACT ONE

SCENE: *A room. The room is in the course of being painted by* TOM. *The distribution of the paint is determined by the way the light falls. There is a window Up Left in the back wall and another Down Right. The paint is darkest where the shadows are darkest and light where they are most light. The painting is not smooth, pretty or finished, but fierce and determined. Onstage there is a stepladder, a divan, two simple wooden chairs; a pair of chest expanders.*

AT RISE: TOM *onstage* U. S. R. *on ladder. Paints out remaining bit of wall paper by painting in an ever smaller circle. Crosses* D. S., *surveys his work. Crosses back onto ladder touches up wall, crosses to clean water on fireplace. Crosses back to ladder, drags it* D. S. *to fireplace. Climbs up to paint above fireplace. Sound of* COLIN *dragging bed downstairs with great clatter as he drops and falls over* TOM'S *things stacked in hall.* COLIN *shoves dresser and chair out of doorway and off* L. *Enters eating raisins from box.*

COLIN. (*Crosses* L.) Er . . . I . . . er . . .
TOM. Fabulous. It's fabulous. It's fantastic.

(*Pause.*)

COLIN. (*Crosses* U. L.) Er . . .
TOM. Is it dry yet?
COLIN. (*Crosses to* L. *wall.*) Where?

TOM. Anywhere.
COLIN. (*Tries.*) Getting on.
TOM. (*Crosses* D. R.) Good. (*Surveys work. Pause.*)
COLIN. I . . . er . . .
TOM. (*Crosses* L., U. S. *of divan on lines.*) I hate that divan. (*Pause.*) More white there perhaps. More white. (*Pause.*) Here. How does the light fall?
COLIN. (*Crosses* U. L.) Eh?
TOM. (*Crosses* L.) The light. Get with it. (*Points out system on wall.*) White where it's light, black where it's dark, grey in between. (*Pause.*)
COLIN. (*Crosses* U. C.) Oh yes . . . yes.
TOM. (*Crosses* R., *up onto ladder.*) Yes? Good. More white. (*He takes a brush of black paint and paints a great black streak on white wall.*) Blast. (*He gets a rag, looks at wall, considers it and then starts working black paint into a painting.*) Yes? Yes? Yes?
COLIN. It's not in the system.
TOM. Eh?
COLIN. (*Points it out to him.*) White where it's light, black where it's dark.
TOM. It's nice. I like it.
COLIN. You're so messy. Everything's messed. It's so badly done.
TOM. I'm not, I'm not a decorator. It looks different, yes?
COLIN. Different?
TOM. Yes.
COLIN. To what?
TOM. To before I moved in. (*Pause.*) He won't like it.
COLIN. Who won't?
TOM. It'll annoy him. It'll annoy Tolen. It'll enrage him.
COLIN. The house doesn't belong to Tolen.
TOM. He'll say it's childish.
COLIN. (*Turns* D. S.) It's my house. (*Crosses* R.) I rent it, so it's mine. (*Pause.*) There's a lot of stuff in the passage.

TOM. Ha, ha! Because Tolen didn't think of it first.

COLIN. The passage is all bunged up. I want to bring my bed downstairs. (*Crosses to* TOM *on ladder.*)

TOM. What's Tolen's first name?

COLIN. He says he hasn't got one.

TOM. Not got one?

COLIN. He never uses it. (*Crosses* U. L. *of divan.*) I want to bring my bed—

TOM. If he never uses it—

COLIN. —my bed downstairs.

TOM. He must have it.

COLIN. I want to bring my bed— (*Sits* D. L. *end of divan.*)

TOM. Well, bring it down! What?

COLIN. I can't get it out of the front door.

TOM. You want to bring your bed—?

COLIN. (*Rises.*) There's too much stuff in the passage.

TOM. I put the stuff in the passage.

COLIN. (*Crosses* D. L.) There's a chest of drawers behind the front door. You can't get out.

TOM. Or in. Where's Tolen?

COLIN. (*Crosses* L. *of door.*) Out. (*Pause.*) Seeing a girl.

TOM. Oh.

COLIN. (*Turns back to* TOM.) There's too much stuff in the passage.

TOM. Why do you want to bring your bed downstairs?

COLIN. (*Crosses* U. L. *of divan.*) The wardrobe and the chest of drawers. We'll bring them in here.

TOM. What!

COLIN. Temporarily.

TOM. No.

COLIN. So I can get the bed through the front door.

TOM. (*Painting.*) We'll bring the bed in here and take it out through the window. (*Slight pause.*)

COLIN. You only put the wardrobe outside while you were painting.

Tom. (*Crosses c., u. s. of divan.*) I don't want it back. The room's so beautiful.

Colin. (*Crosses L.*) But you must be practical—

Tom. (*Gives divan a kick.*) This blasted thing—

Colin. You've got to sit—

Tom. (*Crosses u. c.*) The bottom's falling out.

Colin. You've got to sleep—

Tom. Chairs!

Colin. You can't sleep on the floor. Chairs?

Tom. On the floor. Sleep on it! I think I'll put the mattress on the floor! (*Crosses to divan, grabs mattress.*) Yes! The mattress on the floor. (*Throws mattress on floor D. S. of divan.*) An empty—an empty beautiful room! What an angle! Look! Upwards! What an idea! (*Crosses D. R.*) You marvel, you! (*Seizes D. R. chair. Hoists chair to wall-papered wall.*) On the wall! Out of the way! Off the floor! (*Holding chair to wall.*) I'll hang them on the wall!

Colin. Oh no!

Tom. (*Puts chair back.*) Oh yes! Help! You! (*Crosses to divan.*) Come on! Help me! (*Starts pushing divan to door.*) Help me! Colin! My God, what a splendid idea!

Colin. There's too much stuff in the passage.

Tom. Put it in the basement.

Colin. We haven't got a basement.

Tom. (Colin *puts raisin box by water pipe.* Tom *takes* L. *end of divan, dragging* L.) Give it to Tolen! Put it in Tolen's room! Yes! Come on, help me! (Tom *lets go of divan as* Colin *struggles on—turns to survey work.*) Oh! A beautiful empty room! Why do you want to bring your bed downstairs? (*Crosses back to divan.*)

Colin. Getting another.

Tom. Oh?

Colin. A bigger one. Six foot.

Tom. (*Pause.*) Let's get this shifted. (*They shove divan into hall,* Colin *tugging* U. S., Tom *pushing* D. S.)

Colin. Hadn't we better bring mine in first?

Tom. Into the basement. Give it to Tolen.

(*Noise, off, of MOTOR BIKE which shudders to a stop outside the front door.* TOM *and* COLIN *leave divan leaning against wardrobe and* R. *wall in hallway.*)

COLIN. We haven't got a basement.
TOM. Tolen. That's his motor bike.

(*Great clatter and bang Offstage as they try to clear bed,* TOM'S *furniture, etc. to get front door unblocked. Sound of* SOMEBODY *trying front door.*)

COLIN. It's Tolen. He can't get in. (*Shouting.*) Be with you. (*CLATTER through all of this. Exit* TOM *and* COLIN *with divan. Enter* TOLEN *through window Upstage; takes off sun glasses and coolly surveys room.* COLIN *appears at window.*) Not there.
TOM. (*Off.*) What?
COLIN. He's disappeared. (COLIN *disappears* L.)
TOM. (*Off.*) That's odd.

(*Enter* TOM *through door, as* TOLEN *is cleaning his jacket of dust, followed by* COLIN. TOLEN *does not see* TOM.)

COLIN. Oh there you are.

(TOM *turns to* COLIN *to shut him up as* TOLEN *turns to them.* TOM *bows as if to say, "What do you think?"*)

TOLEN. (*Crossing* D. R. *on* TOM'S *bow.*) Your windows are rather dirty.
TOM. Let's wash them.
COLIN. I—I've got some Windolene. (*Exits into hall.*)
TOM. (*As* COLIN *exits.*) What's that?
COLIN. (*Off.*) For cleaning windows.

(*CLATTER and BANG off as* COLIN *passes through into hall off. Pause. Re-enter* COLIN *with Windolene which he hands to* TOM.)

TOM. (*Reading label,* C.) Wipe it on Windolene, Wipe it off window clean. (*Crosses* U. C. *to window. He wipes some of the Windolene on the bottom half of the window.* COLIN *crosses* U. S. *of* TOLEN *to window.*)

TOLEN. (*As* TOM *wipes Windolene on second pane,* TOLEN *crosses* U. S. *to* D. S. *edge of fireplace.*) Washing with clean water and then polishing with newspaper would have less electro-static action.

COLIN. Oh?

TOLEN. Would repel dirt more efficiently. (TOM *draws three "O" and a straight line on the pane he smeared first. He looks at* COLIN, *pauses, then draws two curved lines to make arms and legs. He looks at* COLIN. COLIN *leans forward, makes a dot for a navel in the middle,* TOM *makes mouth, nipples in two circles, and hair in a beehive around head, then crosses* D. S. *toward next window. As* TOM *crosses to* D. R. *window* TOLEN *stops him.*) Now you must do the top half, Tom. (TOM *pauses, turns, crosses* U. C., *hoists the bottom half of the window up and crosses back to window* D. R., *puts on the Windolene there.*) You do realize, Tom, that in order to clean the window, you have to wipe off the Windolene? (*Pause. As* TOM *turns from window.*) The white stuff has to be polished off the window.

TOM. (*Crossing* C.) Let's get that bed down, shall we, Colin?

COLIN. You can't leave that stuff on.

TOM. (*Stopping* L. *of* COLIN.) Oh?

TOLEN. (*Crossing to* D. R. *window, picks up bottle. Crosses to* R. *of* COLIN, *reading label.*) You can't leave it on. "Wipe on sparingly with a damp cloth and wipe off immediately."

TOM. It's as good as net curtains, only better.

COLIN. (*Takes bottle.*) Net curtains?

TOM. You should paint your windows white, Tolen. White reflects heat. You'll be O.K. when the bomb drops. (*Speaking as he crosses to* L. *door.*)

COLIN. What? What did you say?

TOM. (*CLATTER and BANG off, as if* TOM *were shifting things in hall to get to* COLIN's *bed.*) O.K. when the bomb drops. O.K. when the—
COLIN. Net curtains? (*Exits.*)

(TOLEN *is about to exit when he notices he has Windolene on his hands. He picks up rag on mantel to wipe it off but instead smears them with black paint. The following dialogue continues from* COLIN's *exit with much CLATTER and BANGING under it until we hear the whole bed fall apart on "The head! Hold the head! The head!"*)

COLIN. (*Off.*) It won't go round.
TOM. (*Off.*) It will.
COLIN. (*Off.*) It won't. Take it apart.
TOM. (*Off.*) What?
COLIN. (*Off.*) Take it to bits.
TOM. (*Off.*) Oh all right.
COLIN. (*Off.*) Can you take the head?
TOM. (*Off.*) The what?
COLIN. (*Off.*) The head! Hold the head! The head!
TOM. (*Off.*) Help!
COLIN. (*Off.*) Mind the plaster. (*CRASH Off.*) Oh!
TOM. (*Off.*) You're so houseproud.

(*Enter* COLIN *with head of bed.* COLIN *is about to lean head against wall.*)

TOM. (*Off.*) Not where it's wet! Fool! (*Great CLATTER and BANGING as we hear* TOM *trying to untangle the remains of the bed and himself.* COLIN *leans head of bed against step-ladder* U. R. *CRASH Off.*) Help! Help! I'm stuck! (*Laughing.*) I'm stuck! The foot!
COLIN. The what?
TOM. (*Off.*) The foot!
COLIN. Your foot! (*Exit* COLIN.)
TOM. (*Off.*) Of the bed.

(*BANGING and CRASHING Off with various imprecations. Enter* COLIN *with foot of bed. He crosses* R., *leans it on ladder.*)

TOLEN. Have there been any telephone calls?
COLIN. (*Crossing* L. *to* TOLEN.) Eh?
TOLEN. I'm expecting a couple of girls to telephone.
COLIN. There was a Maureen and er—a Joan.
TOLEN. Joan? Joan who? (COLIN *is nonplussed.*) Never mind, she'll telephone again. (*Pause.* COLIN *crosses* L. *as if to leave.*) I was afraid it was the barmaid at the "Sun."
COLIN. (*In doorway, turns back to* TOLEN.) Alice?
TOLEN. She took me into the little back room this morning.
TOM. (*Entering.*) What about Jimmy?
TOLEN. Probably at Chapel.
TOM. (*Crosses* C.) On Saturday? (*Crosses to ladder, climbs up and begins painting.*)
TOLEN. She said he was at Chapel. Beyond that bead curtain you know, there's a room full of silver cups. Cases of them. And a large pink sofa in the middle. I never knew Jimmy was a sporting man. (*Goes to door.*)
COLIN. (*Counters* R., *stops him.*) Who was the other one?
TOLEN. (*Turns back to* COLIN.) The other?
COLIN. The one you were expecting to telephone.
TOLEN. Girl I met in a telephone kiosk.

(*Exit* TOLEN. *As* COLIN *crosses to mattress, drags it* U. S. *two feet, small CRASH Off. Re-enter* TOLEN.)

TOLEN. (*At door.*) Colin, would you mind moving that bed? I would like to get up to my room.
COLIN. (*Drops mattress, exiting.*) Oh, the base. Sorry.
TOM. Can't you climb over?

(*CRASHING sounds Off.*)

COLIN. (*Off.*) Give me a hand, will you?

Tom. Why can't Tolen?
Colin. Eh? (*Continued CRASHING sounds Off.*)
Tom. It's him that wants to get upstairs.
Colin. Oh, er— (*Re-enters, dragging base.*)
Tom. Mind the paint.

(Colin *drags springs* c., *drops them on top of mattress.*)

Tolen. (*Crosses* l. c.) Why are you bringing your bed downstairs, Colin?

(Tom *stops painting, sits on top of ladder listening.*)

Colin. Getting a new one.
Tolen. Oh?
Colin. A bigger one—six foot.
Tolen. Oh, like mine.
Colin. I—er—I thought—I thought I'd like another one. You know—er—bigger. Just—just in case, you know. (*Gets his foot caught in spring, untangles himself.*) I thought I'd like a bigger—another bed—more comfortable. (*Pause. Crosses* d. r. *on line.*) I could always put my married cousins up. (*Sits on window seat.*)
Tolen. (*Long pause. Crosses* c.) Have you got a girl yet, Colin?
Colin. No.
Tolen. Carol left six months ago, didn't she?
Colin. Mm.
Tom. (*Rises on ladder.*) Have you got a girl yet, Colin?

(Tolen *crosses* u. r.)

Colin. No.
Tom. Got a woman?
Colin. No.
Tom. You haven't, have you?
Colin. No.
Tom. You haven't!

COLIN. No.

TOM. You haven't! You haven't! (*Kicks head and foot of bed that are leaning on the ladder, onto the floor.*) You fool! Why d'you want another bed? (*Climbs down, crosses to bed pieces.*)

COLIN. Mind my bed!

TOM. (*Picks up head of bed.*) His bed! Colin's bed!

COLIN. It's not strong.

(*Through the next lines, TOM crosses D. S. to COLIN, shoving the head of the bed at him, circles L. around mattress and spring, chasing COLIN all the way around and back to L. where COLIN trips and falls over chair. Chair goes against wall. COLIN falls U. S., head of bed falls D. S. of door, TOM falls against L. wall.*)

TOM. (*Through bars of bed.*) Grr! Grr!

COLIN. Hey! Stop! Stop it!

TOM. It creaks! It runs! It spins! Watch it! Yahoo!

COLIN. You'll—

TOM. Poop-poop—

COLIN. I say—

TOM. Poop poop poop poop—

COLIN. Stop it. Stop it.

TOM. Poop poop. Look out!

COLIN. Stop stop—ow! (*Everything collapses.*) You—you—you nit.

(*Pause.*)

TOLEN. (*At window.*) Did you put turpentine in the white?

TOM. Eh?

TOLEN. The white paint. Did you put turpentine in the white?

TOM. (*Sits up on floor.*) Yes.

TOLEN. It'll go yellow.

COLIN. What? (*Rises.*)

TOLEN. The white paint will go yellow.
COLIN. Yellow!
TOLEN. Yes.
COLIN. I never knew that. (*Crosses to box of raisins at pipe.*)
TOLEN. The turpentine thins the white lead in the paint and the linseed oil seeps through and turns the white yellow.

(TOM *rises, crosses* U. S. *to box on floor.*)

COLIN. Oh. D'you think we should do it again? (*Eating raisins.* TOM *is pulling at the chest expanders.*)
TOM. Peter left these, wasn't it nice of him?

(*A* GIRL *passes the window.* TOLEN *exits through window.*)

COLIN. Where are you going? Where— (*Crosses to window, sticks his head out to see what* TOLEN'S *up to. Turns back to* TOM.) How does he do it?
TOM. (*Crosses* U. L. *of window.*) He's beginning to wear out my window. (*Drops expanders* L. *in box.*) Let's move the chest of drawers— (*Turns back to* COLIN.) so he can come in through the front door. (*Taps* COLIN *on shoulder to get his attention.*) He doesn't actually do them in the street, you know.
COLIN. (*Turns to look at* TOM.) Doesn't he?
TOM. (*Crossing* D. L. *to door, picks up head of bed.*) He makes his contact and stashes them up for later. He's enlarging his collection.
COLIN. How does he meet them? (*Stands up at window.*)
TOM. Your bed's in the way. What are we going to do with this bed? What you going to do with it?
COLIN. Oh that. Oh—what's the use? (TOM *lugs head of the bed across and leans it against* COLIN *at window. He crosses* R., *picks up foot and leans it against* COLIN.) What's Tolen got that I haven't got? Maureen says

Tolen's got sexy ankles. (TOM *crosses* D. S. *to* R. *of bedspring and mattress.*) Are my ankles sexy?

TOM. What are you going to do with this bed?

COLIN. Thought I'd take it round to Copp Street.

TOM. Copp Street?

COLIN. To the junk yard.

TOM. To sell?

COLIN. I thought so.

TOM. For money?

COLIN. Why not?

TOM. (*Picks up bedspring, stands it on end.*) O.K. We'll take it round to Copp Street. (*Starts to cross* D. L.) How far is it to Copp Street?

COLIN. Twenty minutes. (*The bed is too heavy,* TOM *puts it down on end, balancing it.*)

TOM. Twenty minutes? (*Long pause.*) Put it back in your room. (*Pause.* COLIN *shakes his head. Pause.* TOM *opens his mouth to speak.*)

COLIN. (*Interrupting.*) Not in the passage. (*Pause.*)

TOM. Can't you just stand there? You look quite nice really. (*Slight pause.*)

COLIN. Put it together.

TOM. No.

COLIN. If we put it together it'll stand by itself.

TOM. No.

COLIN. On its own feet.

TOM. I can't bear it. (*Pause.*)

COLIN. Take the foot. (TOM *lays the spring back on the mattress, crosses to* COLIN *and takes foot.*)

TOM. (*Peering through the bars, then crosses to foot of mattress* R.) How can you sleep on this? I'd think I was at the zoo.

COLIN. (*Crosses to head of bed,* L.) How d'you get a woman? How can I get a girl?

(*They start to put the bed together.*)

TOM. Do you know why the Duck-billed Platypus can't be exported from Australia?

COLIN. How can I get a woman?

TOM. You think this is going to be a silly story, don't you?

COLIN. Well?

TOM. Because they eat their own weight in worms every day and they starve to death in one and a half hours or something. It's rather a nice object. It's not a nice bed but it's not a bad object. Yes. Look. It's rather nice. (COLIN *picks up mattress, is about to put it on bed when* TOM *sees him and shoves him* U. S.) No!

COLIN. But—

TOM. No.

COLIN. But a mattress naturally goes on a bed.

TOM. (*Crosses* R. *of bed.*) It's not a bed. It's an object. More than that, (TOM *gives the bed a push so that it rolls across the room and hits the* L. *wall.*) it's wheeled traffic. Mm. Not much room, is there? I must get those chairs off the floor. (COLIN *sees his chance and before* TOM *can stop him he throws the mattress on the bed and flops on it.*) Put the mattress in the passage.

COLIN. It's more comfy on the bed.

TOM. Oh, very well. (*He rolls the bed, with* COLIN *on it,* U. R. TOLEN *passes the window.*)

COLIN. Why is Tolen so sexy?

(TOLEN *tries the front door.* TOM *rolls the bed and* COLIN *so that the bed is parallel to* R. *wall and on a level with the ladder at* U. S. *edge of fireplace.* TOLEN *enters by the window.*)

TOM. You were very quick. (*Crosses to* U. C.) Did she repulse you? (*Crosses* L. *to* U. S. *window.*)

TOLEN. No. I'm seeing her later.

TOM. Next time I'll time you.

TOLEN. Next time come and watch me.

(TOM *takes the chest expanders from box* L. *and tries them a few times at* C.)

Tom. I'm getting pretty good. Whew! I can do ten of these. Whew! It's awful!

Tolen. (*Crossing D. L. to chair, puts one foot up on it, posing.*) I can do twenty—but then . . .

Tom. Let's see you.

(Tolen *indicates he is below bothering to use his energy.*)

Colin. I can do twenty as well.

Tom. Let's see you. (*Turns to* Colin u. c. Colin *takes the chest expanders and starts.*) He's bending his elbows, it's easier that way.

Colin. (*Stops bending his elbows and continues.*) Four.

Tom. (*Crossing to bed.*) Tolen.

Tolen. Yes, Tom.

Tom. (*Climbs up on bed.*) Do you think it's a good idea for Colin to buy a six-foot bed? (*Sits on bed headboard.*)

Tolen. Where's he buying it? (*Stands up.*)

Colin. Nine. (*Pause.*) Catesby's.

Tom. (*Flops down on bed.*) Plutocrat.

Tolen. Heal's would have been better.

Colin. Twelve. Eh?

Tolen. Heal's have more experience with beds.

Colin. Expensive. Fourteen.

Tolen. They may be expensive, but they have more experience. You pay for their greater experience.

Tom. Yes, but do you think it's a good idea, a sound idea, ethically, for Colin to buy a six-foot bed when he hasn't got a woman?

Tolen. Rory McBride has an eight-foot bed.

(Colin *stops the exercising.*)

Tom. Don't stop! You have to keep it up the whole time. You're not allowed to stop. How sexy is Rory McBride? Who is he, anyway?

Colin. (*Stopping.*) D'you think—?

Tom. Don't stop!

Colin. (*Continuing.*) D'you think—?

TOM. What?
COLIN. I ought to get an eight-foot bed? (*He stops.*)
TOM. How many?
COLIN. Twenty-four. (*Staggering* R.) Where's the bed?
TOM. You mean the object.

(COLIN *collapses on the* D. S. *end of the bed. A* GIRL *is seen to pass the window. Exit* TOLEN *through window.*)

COLIN. (*Sits up.*) Where's he gone?
TOM. A girl passed by and he went after her.

(*Pause.*)

COLIN. (*Smashes fist into mattress.*) You got a cigarette?
TOM. I thought you didn't smoke.
COLIN. Have you got a cigarette?
TOM. No. (COLIN *collapses in a heap on the bed. Pause.*) Listen, Colin, I've had a new idea for you. (TOM *rises, stands on bed.*) For teaching children about music.
COLIN. Oh—
TOM. Listen! My idea about the chalk—was it a good one?
COLIN. It was all right.
TOM. Did you use it or not? Did you?
COLIN. All right. All right. Just tell me.
TOM. Tolen could help, blast him.
COLIN. How?
TOM. He's a musician. You need his advice. But don't let that bastard near the kids, he'll bully them. Now listen, I been thinking about this. You got a piano? Well, have you? Jesus, the bleeding school wouldn't be furnished without a piano.
COLIN. (*Picking up expanders from bed where he dropped them.*) We've got one.
TOM. Good. Listen, I been thinking about this. Teaching's so intellectual and when it's not intellectual,

it's bossy, or most of it. (TOM *crosses L. off bed.*) The teachers tell the kids everything and all they get is dull little copycats, little automata; dim, limited, and safe— (*Crossing C.*)

COLIN. Oh, get on.

TOM. You get the piano— (*Crossing L. to U. S. chair.*) and you get the kids and you say it's a game see? (*Crossing D. L. to chair.*) "Right," you say, "you're not to look at the keys, 'cos that's cheating."

COLIN. (*Raises up on his elbows.*) Not look—

TOM. If they look at each other playing— (*Crossing C.*) they'll just copy each other. Now, don't put your own brain between them and the direct experience. Don't intellectualize. Let them come right up against it. And don't talk about music, talk about noise.

COLIN. (*Flops back down.*) Noi—

TOM. What else is music but an arrangement of noises? I'm serious. "Now," (*Crossing D. L.*) you say, "one of you come out here and makes noises on the piano." And finally one of them will come out and sort of hit the keys, bang, bang. (COLIN *raises up on his elbows.*) "Right," you say, (TOM *crosses D. L. to U. S. chair.*) "now someone come out and make the same noise."

COLIN. Eh?

TOM. (*Crossing U. S. C.*) The same noise. That's the first step. They'll have to *listen* to see they hit in the same place—and they can do it more or less 'cos they can sort of—you know—clout it in the middle bit. (*Crossing R.*) So next you get them all going round the piano, (*Crosses U. S. of bed, leans on head.*) in a circle, all making the same noise, and they'll love that. When they get a bit cheesed, you develop it. "O.K.," you say, "let's have another noise."

COLIN. (*Sits up a bit more.*) I don't see the point.

TOM. Now listen, this way they'll find out for themselves— (*Crossing U. C.*) give them a direct experience and they'll discover for themselves—all the basic principles of music and they won't shy away—they won't think of it as culture, it'll be pop to them. (TOM *crosses U. S. of bed, makes a kick at* COLIN.) Listen! You, goon, moron, you don't like Bartok, do you?

COLIN. No. (*Lies back against head board.*)

TOM. Don't be so pleased with yourself. (TOM *crosses D. L.*) You don't understand it, your ear's full of Bach, it stops at Mahler. But— (TOM *crosses U. S. on a level with* COLIN.) after a few lessons like this, you play those kids Schoenberg, you play them Bartok. They'll know what he's doing. (TOM *climbs up on bed.*) I bet they will! It'll be rock 'n roll to them. My God, (TOM *climbs from bed onto ladder.*) I ought to be a teacher! (*Sees his painting on wall.*) My God I'm a genius! (*Climbs to top of ladder, sits.*)

COLIN. What about Tolen?

TOM. What about him?

COLIN. You said he could help.

TOM. To borrow his gramophone records.

COLIN. He never lends them, he never lets anyone else touch them. (*Pause.*) It's a good idea.

TOM. Good.

COLIN. Thanks. (*Pause.*) Why do you say Tolen is a bastard?

TOM. (*Eating raisins.*) Be careful. He only dazzles you for one reason. Really, Colin, sex, sex, sex: that's all we ever get from you.

COLIN. It's all right for you and Tolen.

TOM. We're all of us more or less total sexual failures.

COLIN. Tolen isn't a sexual failure.

TOM. He needs it five hours a day, he says.

COLIN. Then he can't be a sexual failure. (*Pause.*) He can't be a sexual failure. (*Pause.*) He can't be a sexual failure having it five hours a day. (*Pause.*) Can he?

(*Long pause.*)

TOM. (*Coming down off ladder and crossing* L.) I don't like that wall. There's something wrong with that wall. It's not right.

COLIN. Can he?

(NANCY *appears outside behind the window* C. *and looks about her.* TOM *sees* NANCY, *crosses to* L. *of window, puts raisins on seat. Tries to get* COLIN'S *attention.*)

TOM. Hm. Colin—
COLIN. Can he?
TOM. Colin.

(NANCY *vanishes.*)

COLIN. (*Looks at* TOM *for first time.*) What?
TOM. (*Crossing* L.) Oh, nothing. What do you think about that wall?
COLIN. Blast the wall! Blast the bloody wall! (*Sits up on* U. S. *end of bed.* NANCY *reappears outside the window.* COLIN *spots* NANCY.) Oh . . . oh . . . oh . . .
TOM. (*Seeing* NANCY, *he crosses to* D. S. *edge of fireplace to hide.*) Speak to her.
COLIN. I—I—

(TOM *sees he can't speak so he shoves the bed with* COLIN *on its* U. S. *end right up to the window.*)

TOM. Ask her the time. Ask her to lend you sixpence.
COLIN. I—I— (*Turns desperately to* TOM.) You—
TOM. Eh?
COLIN. You—please.
TOM. I can't do it for you.

(NANCY *vanishes.* COLIN *turns back to window, sees she's gone, turns back to* TOM *with a hopeless look and collapses.*)

COLIN. Oh—

(*Long pause.*)

TOM. (*Crosses* U. L.) What do you think about that wall?

COLIN. What? Oh . . . it's . . . it's . . . (*Has risen to look. Then in a fit of vexation throws the expanders against* S. L. *wall.*)

(*Pause. Enter* TOLEN *through window.*)

TOM. (S. L. *of* TOLEN.) Someone was riding your motor bike.

TOLEN. What? (*Exits through window.* TOM *crosses to window humming, then to bed, climbs over it and up onto ladder.*)

COLIN. Who was riding his motor bike?

(*Re-enter* TOLEN *through window.*)

TOM. I swear someone was riding your motor bike. (*Pause.*) Well? (TOLEN *crosses* D. L. *to* U. S. *of chair.* TOM *sits on top of ladder, painting more white.*) How long did you take this time?

TOLEN. Did you time me?

TOM. Did you time yourself?

COLIN. (*Lying on bed, facing* TOLEN.) How long did you take?

TOLEN. Not more than about ten minutes.

COLIN. Ten minutes! Only ten minutes! (*Collapses in a heap.*)

TOLEN. (*Crossing* C., *patting hair into place.*) Really, Colin, do you think I'm so clumsy, so vulgar as to do it in the street? I'm meeting her . . . (*Crossing* D. L. *as if to leave.*)

TOM. Ten minutes! Ten minutes from door to door? From start to finish? From hello to goodbye?

COLIN. Ten minutes.

TOM. Ten, Tolen! Ten! Ten minutes! Ten whole minutes! What! (*Rises.*) No! You're slipping, man! You're sliding! You're letting us down! Ten. You can do better than that. Faster, man! (TOM *splashes paint all over* COLIN *and the bed as he hits wall with brush.* COLIN *jumps to* D. S. *end of bed.*) Faster! Faster! Faster!

COLIN. Eh?

TOM. (*Crosses* D. S. *on to the bed through the following.*) Dreams I got for you, Tolen. Dreams and plans I got for you. Four minutes! Get it down to four minutes. Four minute from start to finish—like the four-minute mile. (*Jumps off bed.*)

COLIN. (*Rises up.*) Eh?

TOM. (*Crossing* D. C., U. S. *of* TOLEN.) Heroic! Think! A new series in the Olympic Games!

COLIN. (*Crossing* U. S. *of bed to* L. *of center window.*) Is he joking?

TOM. And then, Tolen, by discipline, by training, by application: three minutes fifty-nine seconds! Three minutes fifty-five! Three minutes fifty! And then—one day—one unimaginable day: three minutes! Three minutes from start to finish! (*Falls to the floor.*)

COLIN. (U. L.) Is it nicer, faster?

TOM. Nice? Nice? Nice? (*Rises to his feet,* C.) That's not the point. My God! (COLIN *crosses* U. S. *of head of bed.*) I'm disappointed in you, Tolen, My God I am! Yes! I am! A man with every advantage, every opportunity, every accoutrement—God's gift to women! (*Crosses to* TOLEN, *who is* L. *of* D. S. *chair, and flings himself down on his knees* R. *of chair as if begging for the women.*) And think of those women, Tolen: waiting to be satisfied—their need, Tolen, their crying need— (*Weeping.*) And with the capacity, with the capacity for, with the capacity for spreading yourself around.

TOLEN. I think you're mad.

TOM. (*Gets to feet, crosses* L. *to* TOLEN, *man to man.*) Ah, Tolen, never mind. Relax. I see what you mean. I understand. (*Slight pause.*) You couldn't do it. (*Slight pause.*) You couldn't keep it up. You couldn't keep up the pace. (TOLEN *crosses* R.) Nobody could. It's too much. It's too fast. It's not human, it's superhuman. No, no, let's forget it. Let's be generous. I understand—I'm a man too. (TOM *crosses* R. *as* TOLEN *lies on bed, his head* D. S.) Hah! (*To* COLIN.) He's tired. He's weary.

He's overdone it. Poor chap. He's tired. Quick. Quick. (TOM *crosses* D. L., *shoving* COLIN *almost out the door.* COLIN *protests all the way as* TOM *shouts.* TOM *crosses* U. S. *to the window, sticks his head out shouting, crosses* D. L. *to push* COLIN *again as* NANCY *passes window.*) Blankets! Brandy! Pills! Pillows! Nurses! Stretchers! Doses! Nurses! Nurses! Hot water bottles! Nurses! Nurses! Nurses! Nurses! Have a piece of barley sugar. (NANCY *appears at window.* TOLEN *takes notice.* COLIN *takes notice.* NANCY *disappears.* TOM *turns from* COLIN, *sees* TOLEN *cross to window, rushes to stop him, kneels in front of him pleading.*) Save yourself! Control yourself! Give yourself a chance!

(TOLEN *shoves him over and looks out window;* COLIN *at* L. *also looks out at* NANCY.)

TOLEN. A bit provincial. (*Turns back into room* U. S. *of* TOM *lying on floor.*)
TOM. (*Raises his head.*) What?
TOLEN. That girl. A bit provincial.
TOM. (*Really wanting to know.*) How can you tell she's provincial?
TOLEN. (*Crossing* D. S., *looks down into* TOM'S *face.*) Of course, Tom, you will not appreciate that the whole skill, the whole science, is in the slowness: the length of time a man may take. The skill is in the slowness. Of course, Tom, I don't expect you can appreciate this. There is little skill, Tom, (COLIN *crosses to* L. *of* TOLEN *above* TOM.) and no subtlety in the three-minute make. However—
COLIN. It's better slower?

(TOM *and* TOLEN *both turn to stare at this bit of idiocy.* COLIN *retreats into* U. L. *corner.*)

TOLEN. (*Crosses to* C.) However, if I wished, Tom, if I wanted, you do realize that I could do it in about eighty-five seconds? (*He crosses* D. L. *as if to leave.*)

Tom. Yes.

Colin. (*Crosses* D. L. *and gets between* Tolen *and the door to stop him.*) Tolen.

Tolen. (*Stops.*) Yes, Colin?

Colin. Will you—I mean—will you show me— (*Pause.*) how? (*Pause.*)

Tolen. You mean how I get women?

Colin. Yes.

Tolen. I can tell you what I know intellectually, Colin, what my experience has been. But beyond that it's a question of intuition. (Tom *picks himself up off floor and crosses* U. S. *to ladder.*) Intuition is, to some degree, inborn, Colin. One is born with an intuition as to how to get women. (Colin *thinks he means it's hopeless and turns to go.*) But— (*This stops* Colin *and he turns back.*) this feeling can be developed with experience and confidence, in certain people, Colin, to some degree. A man can develop the knack. First— (Tom *gives the ladder a violent jerk and begins to drag it across to* L. Tolen *stops as ladder makes a great clatter. As* Tom *continues* L., Tolen *trailed by* Colin *crosses* U. R. *of bed, as* Tom *drags ladder to pipe. As* Tolen *and* Colin *reach* U. R. *of bed,* Tom *is about six feet from the wall.* Colin *can't stand it and crosses to* Tom, *jerks the ladder off the floor, and they silently carry it into place at the pipe.* Tom *nods his thanks,* Colin *glares at him, turns, crosses back to* Tolen *to hear the rest of what he has to say.* Tolen *starts to speak,* Tom *gives the ladder a violent jerk.* Tolen *and* Colin *turn as if to say "Do you mind?"* Tom *ignores them, tiptoes to the top of the ladder, sits down facing them to listen, then nods as if to say "You may proceed."* Tolen *continues his lecture.*) You must realize that women are not individuals but types. No, not even types, just women. They want to surrender but they don't want the responsibility of surrendering. This is one reason why the man must dominate. (Colin *smashes his fist into his palm.*) On the other hand there are no set rules. A man must be infinitely subtle; must use his intuition, a very subtle intuition. (TOLEN *crosses* D. S. COLIN *counters*.) If you feel it necessary in order to get the woman you must even be prepared to humiliate yourself, (TOLEN *sits on* U. R. *edge of bed,* COLIN *sits at his feet*.) to grovel, to utterly abase yourself, before the woman—I mean only in cases of extreme necessity, Colin. After all, what does it matter? It's just part of getting her. Once you've got her it's the woman that grovels. Finally, Colin, the man is the master. For you must appreciate, Colin, that people like to be dominated. They like to be mastered. They ask to be relieved of the responsibility of deciding for themselves. It's a kindness towards people to relieve them of responsibility. In this world, Colin, there are the masters and there are the servants. Very few men are real men, Colin, are real masters. Almost all women are servants. They don't want to think for themselves, they want to be dominated. (TOLEN *rises, crosses* C., COLIN *counters*.) First you must establish contact. Of course you won't find that as easy as I do. I'm not referring to touch, tactile communications, that comes later. I mean the feeling between you. You are aware of the girl, the girl is aware of you, a vibration between you—

COLIN. Just a minute.
TOLEN. Yes?
COLIN. I just want to get it straight.
TOLEN. Take your time.

(*Pause.*)

COLIN. (*Sits* U. R. *edge of bed.*) I don't see what you mean by contact.

TOLEN. Very difficult to explain. (TOLEN *turns away, sees* TOM *staring at his performance, crosses to* TOM.) Tom, can you explain?

TOM. No.

TOLEN. (*Crosses to* COLIN.) Once you feel it, Colin, you will know it next time. (*Turns back in to lecture, crosses to* C.) Having established this basis of contact, then you work to break down her resistance, to encourage surrender. Flattery is useful; if a woman is intelligent make her think she's pretty, if she's pretty make her think she's beautiful. Never let them think— (*Crossing u. s. c.*) never let them see you are clever or intellectual. Once you let a woman start thinking, the whole process takes infinitely more time. Keep her laughing, keep her talking; (*Crossing R. to* COLIN.) you can judge by her laughter, by the way she laughs, how you're getting on. (TOLEN *tickles* COLIN, COLIN *giggles, then tickles back. There is an awkward moment—*TOLEN *is not amused.*) Perhaps it might be useful to consider what is the right food.

COLIN. The right food?

TOLEN. Food is of the utmost importance. (*Crosses c.*) Food is of the essence. One's body needs protein and energy-giving substance. I find with my perhaps unusual sexual demands that my body requires at least twice the normal daily intake of protein.

COLIN. Protein?

TOLEN. (*Crossing R. to* COLIN.) Cheese, eggs, milk, meat. I drink about four pints of milk a day—Channel Island milk. And eat about a pound of steak. It needn't be the most expensive, the cheaper cuts have the same food value. For instance, tail.

TOM. Tail? (*Giggling into shirt.*)

TOLEN. (*Turns to* TOM.) Tail.

COLIN. Tail. (*Rises, crosses to* TOM *on ladder.*) Cheese, eggs, milk, meat, tail. Got a pencil, Tom?

TOLEN. Tail is meat.

COLIN. Oh.

TOM. (*Rises and stands on ladder.*) Don't you see what you're doing to this growing lad? He hasn't got a woman, now he'll go and eat himself silly on milk and meat, Stoke up the fire and block up the chimney. (TOM *runs down the ladder and crosses to* D. R. *end of bed.*) Listen, Colin, suppose this was a piano. (TOM *pulls up chair to* D. R. *edge of bed and sits as if to play.*)

ACT I   THE KNACK

TOLEN. (*Crossing* D. L.) A what?
COLIN. (*To* TOM.) Shut up.
TOM. A piano. Plonk, plonk, plonk.
TOLEN. (*At* D. L. *door.*) It's a bed.
TOM. It's not, it's a piano, listen.
COLIN. (*Crosses* D. R. *to* TOM.) I want Tolen to tell me—
TOM. Shut up, he's told you enough. A piano, plonk. Now supposing you couldn't—
COLIN. (*Crossing* L. *to* TOLEN.) Listen, Tolen—
TOM. Supposing you couldn't see my hand—
COLIN. (*Crossing* R. *to* TOM.) Shut up.
TOM. I play—C-sharp, F and A—
COLIN. (*Crosses* L. *to* TOLEN.) Tolen— (TOM *tries to interrupt through all of this.*) I want—listen to me. I want to hear what—I want to hear what Tolen has to say. Listen—listen to me. I want to hear wh-what Tolen has to say. So *what* you think it's b-bad for me to listen to Tolen. You're not in charge of me. I am and I'm sick of myself, I'm absolutely sick, (TOM *is finally silenced.*) and here I am stuck with myself. I want to hear what Tolen has to say— (NANCY *re-appears, knocks on window.*) I want to hear what Tolen has to say.
NANCY. Do you know where I can find the Y.W.C.A.?

(*Pause.*)

TOM. The what?
NANCY. The Y.W.C.A.

(*Pause.*)

TOM. Come on in. (NANCY *starts to hoist bags right in the window.*) Come in by the front door.
NANCY. Oh thanks. Thanks very much.

(NANCY *disappears* L. *The* BOYS *look at each other a moment.* TOM *exits. Great CLATTER and BANG off as he moves things to get to front door. Meanwhile,* TOLEN, D. C., *pats his hair, tucks his shirt in tight, as* COLIN, U. R., *tries to copy what he's doing. Enter* NANCY *carrying a handbag and a shopping bag,* TOM *a large suitcase.*)

NANCY. Hullo. (TOM *puts the bag down.*)
TOLEN. Hullo.
COLIN. Oh, hullo.

(*Pause.* TOM *leans against foot of bed.*)

TOM. Well, has anyone seen it?
COLIN. (*Crosses* D. S. *to* U. S. *end of bed.*) Seen what?
NANCY. The Y.W.C.A.
TOM. The Y.W.C.A.
COLIN. Oh, the Y.W.C.A.
TOM. Yes.
COLIN. No.

(*Pause.* TOM, *trying to cover, leaps* R. *and grabs chair.*)

TOM. Would you like to sit down? (*Crosses* L. *and places chair for* NANCY.)
NANCY. Well, thanks, but—but well, thanks. (*She puts her bags down, and sits.* TOM *counters to* L. *side of bed.* NANCY *looks at the* BOYS *uncertainly. They all start to advance on her; she starts to panic.*)
TOM. (*Again trying to cover an embarrassing moment.*) Would you like a cup of tea or something?
NANCY. Oh, well, no thanks, really.
TOM. No trouble, it's no trouble. I'll put the kettle on. (*Exits* L.)
TOLEN. (*At* C. *turns to* COLIN.) Did he say he'd put a kettle on? He's not boiled a kettle since he came here.
TOM. (*Off.*) Colin!
COLIN. (*Crossing* C.) Yes?
TOM. (*Off.*) How do you turn the gas on? (*Pause.* TOLEN *now pursues the intention of teasing* NANCY *and*

making her uncomfortable. TOLEN *looks at* COLIN *as if to say,* "*Watch this.*" *He turns and slowly swaggers over to* NANCY *till he is looming over her, then looks down right into her eyes.* NANCY *shudders and leaps for the door as* TOM *enters.*) How do you turn— (COLIN *crosses* U. R., TOLEN D. L. TOM *sizes up what is going on in an instant and again saves it by covering. Runs to* U. R. *to* L. *of bed.*) What do you think of our piano? (*Pointing to bed.*)

NANCY. What?

TOM. Our piano. Do you like it? Our piano?

NANCY. What piano?

TOM. This piano. (*Rolls the bed* D. C., *head* L.)

NANCY. Piano?

TOM. Yes.

NANCY. That's not a piano. (*Not sure if they are insane or what, she retreats toward her bags and the door.*)

TOM. Yes it is, it's a piano.

NANCY. It's a bed.

TOM. It's a piano, honest, listen: ping!

NANCY. It's a bed.

TOM. It's a piano, isn't it, Colin?

COLIN. (*Steps* D. S.) Eh?

TOM. This is a piano.

COLIN. Piano?

TOM. Piano.

COLIN. (*Crosses to* R. *of* TOM *to play piano.*) Oh yes, a piano. Ping.

NANCY. It's a bed.

TOM. (*Using edge of bed as keyboard.*) Ping— (*High.*) ping. (*Low.*) Ping— (*Running his finger right down in a glissando.*) pi-i-i-ing.

COLIN. (*Middle.*) Ping.

NANCY. (*Edging back into room giggling.*) It's a bed.

TOM. (*Kneeling to play.*) Bechstein.

NANCY. (*Crossing to* L. *end of bed.*) Bechstein?

TOM. (*High.*) Ping. (*Medium high.*) Ping. (*Medium low.*) Ping. (*Low.*) Ping.

NANCY. (U. S. *of* L. *end of bed.*) It's a bed.

TOM. (*First bars of "Blue Danube" starting low.*) Ping ping ping ping ping.

NANCY. It's a bed.

COLIN. (*Touching foot of bed as if it was real.*) Rosewood.

TOM. (*"Blue Danube."*) Ping ping, ping ping.

NANCY. It's a bed.

TOM. Ping ping ping ping ping, ping ping—

COLIN. (*Kneels by* TOM *at* R. *end, takes over ninth bar.*) Ping ping.

TOM and COLIN. (*Together playing in unison tenth to thirteenth bars.*)
    Ping ping ping ping ping
    ping ping, ping ping
    ping ping ping ping ping
    ping ping,

(TOM *stops* COLIN *so that* NANCY *has to end phrase.*)

NANCY. Ping ping. (*Kneels at* L. *end of bed.*)

TOM, COLIN and NANCY. Ping ping ping ping ping,
    ping ping, ping ping
    ping ping ping ping ping
    ping ping, ping ping
    ping ping ping ping ping
    ping ping ping
    ping ping ping, pingping, ping ping ping-ping.

TOM. (*Solo on first notes of introduction of middle part.*) PING PING!

TOM, COLIN and NANCY. ping ping ping
    ping ping ping ping ping

(*During middle part,* TOM *rises, crosses* U. S. *to mantel, leaving* COLIN *alone at piano with* NANCY. COLIN *soon realizes he is alone, moves closer to* NANCY *and starts to have a lovely time.*)

NANCY. Ping.
COLIN. Ping.

NANCY. Ping.
COLIN. Ping.
NANCY. Ping.
COLIN. Plong.
NANCY. Plong.
COLIN. Plong plong.
NANCY. Ping plong.
COLIN. Plong.
NANCY. Ping.
COLIN. Ping.
NANCY. Plong.
COLIN. Plong.
NANCY. Plong.
COLIN. Plong.
TOLEN. (*Crosses* D. S C. L. *and kicks the bed.*) Why be so childish about a bed?

(*There is a pause.* NANCY *and* COLIN *become embarrassed,* NANCY *crosses* U. L. *of window and* COLIN *crosses* D. R. *to sit on window seat. Pause as* TOLEN *crosses to chair* D. L. *and sits.* AUTHOR'S NOTE: *All the above could be rearranged or improvised to suit different actors and different productions provided the sequence of events is clear:* 1. TOM *and* COLIN *charm* NANCY *into entering into the game.* 2. TOM *retires, leaving* COLIN *and* NANCY *getting on rather well, a growing relationship which* TOLEN *interrupts.*)

TOM. (*At* U. S. *end of fireplace.*) Would anyone like to know how they train lions to stand on boxes? (*Crossing to* NANCY *at* L. *of window.*) Would you like to know how they train lions to stand on boxes? First we must have a box. (*Crosses* U. R. *to bucket.*) That will do. (*Crosses to bed, rolls it* R. *with head* D. S.) Now this marks the limit of the cage—the edge, the bars.
TOLEN. (*As* TOM *crosses* U. C.) Must you be so childish?
TOM. (*Turns to* TOLEN.) Child*like*. The trainer takes

his whip. Whip? (*Crosses* D. C.) Whip? (*Crosses* U. C.) We'll do without a whip. Now a lion. I must have a lion. (*Crosses to* TOLEN.) Tolen, you'd make a good lion. No? O.K. Colin. (*Crosses to* D. L. *edge of bed.*)

COLIN. No.

TOM. (*Crosses to* COLIN.) Come on, be a lion.

COLIN. No.

TOM. Go on, can't you roar? (*Crossing* U. C.) The trainer taking the box in his left hand, and the whip—imagine the whip in his right, advances on the lion—(*Crossing* D. C.) and drives him backwards against the cage bars, yes? Now. (*Crossing* U. C.) There is a critical moment when the lion must leap at the attacker otherwise it will be too late, see? Right. The trainer can recognize the critical moment. (*Crossing* D. C.) So, at the moment when the lion rears to attack, the trainer—(*Crossing* U. C.) draws back and the lion, no longer threatened, (*Crossing* D. C.) drops his forepaws and finds himself standing on the box. (TOM *bows and sweeps a gesture to* TOLEN *who is sitting on the back of the chair with his feet on the seat very much like a tame lion.*) Do this a few times and you've trained a lion to stand on a box.

(*Pause.*)

COLIN. How does the box get there?
TOM. What?
COLIN. You've still got it in your hand.
TOM. The trainer puts it there.
COLIN. When?

(*Pause.*)

TOM. Let's try. You come and be lion.
COLIN. No.
TOM. All right, I'll be lion. (*Crosses* U. C., *puts bucket under window and begins to imitate a lion roaring at*

NANCY, *meowing like a kitten at* TOLEN. *Crosses to* COLIN, *roars at him, crosses back* U. C.) Whew! It makes you feel sexy. (*Roars again.*)

COLIN. I'd like to be lion. (*Crosses* U. C. *and grabs bucket, roars into it.*)

TOM. That's the lion's box. (*Crosses to* COLIN, *takes bucket, puts it in corner.*)

COLIN. Sounds marvelous inside. (*Sees* NANCY'S *shopping bag; crosses* D. L. *and picks it up.*)

TOM. Hey, you can't touch that. (*Crosses* D. C. *to stop him.*)

COLIN. Eh?

NANCY. Oh, that's all right. (NANCY *crosses to* COLIN, *takes bag, crosses to bed followed by* COLIN. *She empties contents onto bed: three record albums, umbrella and a copy of* Honey *Magazine.* COLIN *puts shopping bag on his head.* NANCY *crosses* D. R. TOM *crosses* D. S. *to* COLIN, *guides him* U. R. *around bed toward* NANCY. COLIN *is roaring like a lion, backs* NANCY D. C.)

TOM. Yes! Yes! Yes! Yes!

(NANCY *laughs, half scared, half excited.* COLIN *roars at her and she runs away* D. C. COLIN *gropes for her, but she evades him laughing.*)

COLIN. Just a minute.

(COLIN *takes bag off his head and makes holes for eyes.*)

TOM. What are you doing?
COLIN. Making eyeholes.

(COLIN *puts bag back on head. Roars again after* NANCY. NANCY *now plays role of trainer; with imaginary whip she drives* COLIN *against the bed.* COLIN *rears back and grabs her, starts to scratch her back and purr.*)

TOLEN. (*Rises. In a loud voice.*) I'll be trainer. (*He whips off his belt for a whip.*)

Tom. Eh? Very well.

Tolen. Ready? (COLIN *releases* NANCY, TOLEN *picks up chair on which he was sitting, like a trainer.* COLIN *crosses* D. L. *to* TOLEN, *roaring. Pause.* TOLEN *advances on* COLIN *cracking his "whip" and getting a sweet pleasure from the identification.* COLIN *roars,* TOLEN *gets more excited and vicious. Starts to hit the chair bottom with the belt, driving* COLIN *into* U. R. *corner.*) Back—back you—back you—back—back, you beast you—beast you beast you back back!

(NANCY *gets mixed up in between them,* TOLEN *turns on* NANCY *with the chair and whip. She screams, exits out the* U. S. *window, and runs screaming Offstage* L. TOLEN *throws the chair down, leaving* COLIN *cowering in the corner.* TOLEN *picks up* Honey. *Pause.*)

Tom. Just think what you could do with a real whip, Tolen. Think of that.

Colin. (*Taking off shopping bag.*) What's happened? Has she gone? (*Looking about in amazement.*)

Tom. (*As he and* COLIN *both spot the suitcases* D. L.) She left her suitcases.

CURTAIN

ACT TWO

The room is very peaceful. TOM *is up on ladder* L., *painting gently and thinking about his paint.* COLIN *has the shopping bag on his head and is feeling free and experimental.* TOM *is painting a black shadow on the wall behind the water pipe.* COLIN *is* D. R., *being a large sailing seagull providing his own sound effects of sea and wind. Crosses* U. R., L. *of bed to* U. S. *of bed. After a long pause.*

TOM. What do you think?

(*Pause.*)

COLIN. Not thinking.

(*Pause.*)

TOM. Eh?
COLIN. Not thinking.

(TOM *turns to* COLIN, *sees he's facing* R.)

TOM. (*Pointing to his work.*) Look!
COLIN. (*Turns to look at painted shadow, takes off bag.*) Oh. (*Crosses* U. C., *puts bag* L. *on window seat. Sits* R. *on window seat, looking out into street.*)
TOM. Ah . . . (*Pause.*) This place soothes me.
COLIN. I remember the first time I saw this street.
TOM. (*Turning to* COLIN.) Northam Street?
COLIN. These mean streets. (TOM *continues his work.*) The feeling of space in these streets—it's fantastic. (*Pause.*) when they're empty they're sort of—splendid, a sort of—crumbling splendor— (*Pause.* COLIN *crosses*

D. R., *sits on bed with his head against the headboard.*) and a feeling of—in winter, on a hazy, winter day a—a —a—romantic! And in summer hot and—listless. And at weekends, summer and the sun shining and children dashing about and mothers talking—you know, gossiping and men cleaning motorbikes and— (*Getting excited.*) they can be forbidding, threatening—I mean—you know—if the light's flat and darkish—no sun—just flat and lowering, it's stupendous! And early morning—early autumn— I've walked through these streets all alone, you know, all by myself—so quiet . . . (*TELEPHONE rings, off.*) It'll be for him, It'll be for Tolen.

(COLIN *puts the shopping bag on his head and picks up a magazine. Exit* TOM. *The TELEPHONE stops ringing. We hear* TOM *in conversation. Pause.* NANCY *appears at the window, she doesn't see* COLIN. NANCY *climbs through the window and goes toward the suitcases.* COLIN *sees* NANCY. NANCY *picks up the suitcases, turns, sees* COLIN *and is transfixed. She drops both suitcases and flattens herself against* L. *wall. Pause. Enter* TOLEN *through window.* TOLEN *crosses* D. S. *to* NANCY. TOLEN *whips off his belt.* NANCY *darts away* D. R. TOLEN *smacks belt on chair and follows.* COLIN *crosses* U. L. NANCY *crosses* U. R., *hysterical. There is a maelstrom of movement during which* TOLEN *turns over the bed, catching* NANCY *behind it in* U. R. *corner.* TOLEN *stands facing her, whip in hand. Enter* TOM *through* L. *door. Pause.*)

TOM. (*At door.*) Colin, take that carrier bag off your head.
COLIN. Eh?
TOM. (*Crossing* U. C.) Take it off. (COLIN *removes bag.* TOLEN *crosses* D. L., *putting his belt on.*) Shall we get the bed straight? (TOM *goes to foot of bed.*) Tolen? (TOM *and* COLIN *put the bed together.* COLIN *puts records jackets on bed.*) You not found the Y.W.C.A.?

NANCY. No.
TOM. (*Adjusting bed.*) What's the address?
NANCY. I've got it here. (*Hands him a scrap of paper.*)
TOM. (*Crossing* C.) Martin's Grove, W. 2. Where's Martin's Grove?
COLIN. (*As he exits* L.) I don't know. I'll get the street map.

(*Pause.*)

NANCY. (*Helping with bed.*) Thanks.
TOLEN. That's all right.
NANCY. Oh, thanks.
TOLEN. Don't mention it.

(*Enter* COLIN *with street guide. Crosses toward* NANCY, *who is* R. *of bed.* TOM *intercepts and takes guide.* TOM *and* COLIN *sit* R. *edge of bed.*)

TOM. How does it work?
COLIN. Index.
TOM. Eh?
COLIN. Back.
TOM. I see.
TOLEN. (*Crosses* U. L. *of bed.*) Just come off the train, have you?
NANCY. Yes.
COLIN. James Park, James Square, turn over, and again. Ah. Mapperton, Marlow.
TOLEN. Is it the—
TOM. Martin's Grove W. 2 J4. 73. What's that?
COLIN. Page seventy-three.
TOLEN. Is it the first time you've been here?
NANCY. Here?
TOLEN. In London?
NANCY. Oh yes.

(TOLEN *and* NANCY *laugh.*)

COLIN. Square J above, 4 across.

TOM. What tiny print.
TOLEN. You've got Chinese eyebows.
NANCY. Eh?
TOLEN. Chinese eyebows. Very clear arch. Very delicate.
NANCY. Have I?
TOLEN. Have you got a mirror, I'll show you. (*Crosses* C.)

(NANCY *crosses* U. R. *around bed to* TOLEN. *He takes mirror and holds it for her.*)

NANCY. Oh.
COLIN. Turn it the other way.
TOM. Eh?
COLIN. Round. That's it.
TOLEN. See? Very pretty.
NANCY. (*Taking mirror, looking at herself.*) Oh.
TOM. (*Rises, crosses to* R. *of* NANCY.) Here. Here it is.
NANCY. Eh? Oh thanks.
TOM. Not far. Five minutes. (NANCY *is occupied with mirror.*) We'll take you. We'll take you there.
NANCY. Oh. Oh thanks. Thanks very much. Well perhaps I ought to— (NANCY *reluctantly crosses to suitcases.* TOM *sees she isn't going.*)
TOLEN. What's your name?
NANCY. (*Glad to be stopped, crosses back to* TOLEN, C. TOM *sees what's coming, crosses to bed and sits back against headboard.* COLIN *takes it all in, "learning."*) Nancy, Nancy Jones. What's yours?
TOLEN. Tolen.
NANCY. Tolen? Tolen what?
TOLEN. Tolen.
NANCY. Tolen, oh I see, like Capucine.
TOLEN. I beg your pardon?
NANCY. Capucine.
TOLEN. Capucine?

NANCY. Like Capucine. Nothing Capucine, Capucine nothing.
TOLEN. Please would you tell me what you mean?
NANCY. You not seen her? She's an actress. She acts.
TOLEN. On television?
NANCY. In the films. Is it your Christian name or your surname? (*Pause.*) Well, is it? Is it your surname or your Christian name?
TOLEN. It's my surname.
NANCY. What's your Christian name?
TOLEN. I never use my first name. I have no first name.
NANCY. What is it?
TOLEN. I prefer not to use it.
NANCY. Why?
TOLEN. I don't use it. I have no first name. I never use my first name. (TOM *and* COLIN *both break up at* TOLEN'S *discomfort. He turns and silences them with a glare—*COLIN *reads the street guide and* TOM *looks down inside his shirt.* TOLEN *then makes a complete circle around* NANCY *to* R. NANCY *shifts uncomfortably.*) What's the matter? Is anything wrong? Is anything the matter with you?
NANCY. No.
TOLEN. Why are you so nervous?
NANCY. I'm not.
TOLEN. You look nervous.
NANCY. Me nervous? Do I?
TOLEN. Yes.
NANCY. Oh—
TOLEN. Yes?
NANCY. Nothing.

(*Through this section* TOLEN *backs* NANCY *to* R. *of door.*)

TOLEN. What's the matter?
NANCY. It's—it's—
TOLEN. Well?

NANCY. It's—
TOLEN. You are nervous, aren't you? Very nervous. Why don't you take your coat off?
NANCY. I don't want to.
TOLEN. My dear, you take it off.
NANCY. I don't want to.
TOLEN. Why don't you want to?
NANCY. No.

(*Exit* COLIN *depressed at* TOLEN'S *power.* NANCY *turns to watch him go out* L. *door. As she turns back to face* TOLEN, *he pounces.*)

TOLEN. Yes?

(*Pause.*)

NANCY. You're looking at me.
TOLEN. Am I?
NANCY. Yes.
TOLEN. How am I looking?
NANCY. I don't know, I—
TOLEN. How am I looking?
NANCY. I—
TOLEN. Well?
NANCY. I feel—
TOLEN. What?
NANCY. I don't know, I feel—
TOLEN. (*Really moves in on her.*) You feel funny, don't you? Go on, tell me—go on—tell me—tell me.

(NANCY *shudders, runs* U. C. *to window.* TOLEN *laughs.*)

TOM. (*Rises, sits on* L. *edge of bed.*) What's the most frightening building in London?
TOLEN. (*Stretching and yawning.*) It depends what you mean by frightening.
TOM. Break it up, Tolen.
TOLEN. What I do is my affair, not yours. (*Crossing* D. L., *adjusting his clothes.*)

Tom. She doesn't know a thing.

Tolen. She knows what she wants, or rather what she will want. (*Sits sprawling arrogantly* D. L. *chair.*)

Tom. I don't think you're the right person to give a girl her first experience.

Tolen. She's an independent human being. Why should you say what's good for her? How old are you, Nancy?

Nancy. Seventeen.

Tolen. There you are. (*Pause.*) Anyway, she's not really my type. I've had sufficient for today. I'm merely amusing myself. It's more subtle.

Tom. (*Rises, crosses* U. C. *to* Nancy.) You know what happens to young girls alone in London, don't you?

Nancy. Yes—no—I—

Tom. (*Crosses to ladder* L. *and climbs up to continue painting.*) You'd better find a Catholic girl's refuge.

Nancy. I'm not a Catholic.

Tom. You'll find the address in any ladies' lavatory in any railway station.

Nancy. Oh—I—

Tolen. How do you know?

(*CLATTER and BANG Off as* Colin *bashes into furniture in hall.*)

Nancy. I think I ought to go—I—

(*Enter* Colin *with tea things including milk in a bottle, through door. Crosses* R. *of* Tom, *who is still on the ladder.*)

Colin. That damned stuff in the passage. You'll have to move it.

Tom. I'm not having it in here.

Colin. I'm not having it in the passage.

Tom. I'm not having it in here.

Colin. (*Yelling at* Tom—*who is yelling right back— and trying to find a place to put down the tray.*) When you take a furnished room, you take the furniture as well.

Tom. Not that furniture.

Colin. What's wrong with the furniture?

Tom. I'm not having it in here. Put it on the bed. Take it to Copp Street.

Colin. It's my furniture, you're not selling my furniture.

Tom. You're selling your bed.

Colin. You're not selling my furniture.

Tom. We'll put it on the top landing.

Tolen. Outside my room? I think not.

Tom. Inside your room.

Colin. (*Putting tea tray on floor L. of bed.*) Oh. Let's have some tea.

(Colin *crosses* D. L. *to chair, places it for* Nancy U. R. *of tray. Squats* L. *of tray, begins to pour tea.* Tolen *crosses to bed, sits* U. S. *edge next to* Nancy. *He starts to fix a cup of tea, which* Nancy *thinks is for her.* Tolen *drinks it.* Colin *hands cup of tea to* Nancy.)

Tolen. What's the most frightening building in London?

Colin. Great Ormond Street Hospital for Children.

(*Pause.*)

Tom. (*On ladder.*) What's that?

Colin. (*Turning to* Tom.) Great Ormond Street Hospital for Children.

Nancy. That's nice. It's true That's a nice thing to say.

Colin. Oh! Do you think so?

(Tolen *touches* Nancy *and distracts her attention from* Colin.)

Tom. (*Trying to cover the moment and distract*

TOLEN.) Do you know how the elephant got the shape it is? Well, (TOM *climbs down off ladder.*) there once was a little piggy animal, see? (NANCY *gets sugar for tea.*) With two great big front teeth that stuck out. (TOM *crosses* U. C.) However, there are certain advantages in being big— (COLIN *sits on floor* L. *of tray.*) you know, (TOM *crosses* U. S. *of bed.*) you can eat off trees and things—like horses—

TOLEN. For you this is remarkably incoherent.

TOM. Thanks. (*Climbs up onto bed,* U. S. *end.*) So this animal got big and grew an enormous great long jaw so it could scoop up the vegetation. (*Sits on headboard.*) An enormous jaw, seven foot long—imagine! As big as a door! Now. A seven-foot jaw involves certain difficulties in getting the food from the front of your jaw to the back . . .

TOLEN. (*Picking up saucer, offers to* NANCY *and* COLIN. NANCY *takes one.*) Biscuits?

TOM. It had to use its upper lip to shovel the garbage along.

COLIN. Aren't there some chocolate? (TOLEN *puts saucer back on tray.*)

TOM. I ate them. Well, (*Stands ups.*) the creature's upper lip began to grow. It grew so big it began to do all the work and the creature didn't bother to use its seven-foot jaw. Now, as you know, any organ not in constant use atrophies. So the jaw began to shrivel. (*To* TOLEN.) Not that you need . . .

NANCY. Tea?

TOM. *But* the two front teeth— (*Sits on* D. S. *end of bed.*)

NANCY. More tea?

TOM. Remained. So you are left with an animal having an extraordinarily long upper jaw and two big front teeth. You're left with an elephant. (TOM *rises, steps off bed and crosses* U. S. *around* COLIN.) No problem at all. Yes, I would, please.

(NANCY *pours tea for* TOM. TOLEN *touches* NANCY'S *arm.* NANCY *thinks he is admiring her slicker.*)

NANCY. D'you like it? It's new. (TOLEN *is amused and pleased at* NANCY'S *obvious inexperience.* NANCY *is quiet, happy to settle down for a nice cup of tea, and starts to take off her coat to stay a while.*)

TOLEN. You should paint that wall straight away or it'll patch up. (*Puts his tea cup down, swings his legs onto the bed.*)

TOM. What?

TOLEN. It will dry blotchy.

TOM. Yes. That's a good idea. Yes!

TOLEN. You wanted to see me? (TOLEN *adjusts himself on bed.*)

COLIN. Eh?

TOLEN. That's right. (*Leans back against headboard.*)

COLIN. Wanted to see you?

TOLEN. You will. (*Reaches down to foot of bed for* "Honey" *magazine.*)

COLIN. What d'you—

TOLEN. (*Returns to position against headboard.*) Watch this.

COLIN. What do you mean?

TOM. (*Backing to ladder.*) In cold blood, Colin, in cold blood.

TOLEN. I'll show you how.

(*It dawns on* COLIN *what* TOLEN *is talking about. He leaps to his feet as if stung and retreats fascinated to* L. *of window, where he remains looking on, riveted to the scene.*)

TOM. (*Angry.*) Nancy! You should go when you're told.

(NANCY *looks around uncertainly to see what is going on*

and rises reluctantly to leave. TOLEN *moves as if he is uncomfortable.* NANCY *sees a chance to stay.*)

NANCY. Would you like something behind your head?
TOLEN. There is a pillow in the passage.

(NANCY *exits, passes the pillow on the hall chair. We hear CLATTER and BANG Off as she looks for pillow. As this goes on,* TOLEN *gives* COLIN *a look of triumph, reaches down, shoves tea tray under edge of bed, grabs chair* NANCY *has been sitting on, pulls it smack up against bed and moves over on bed right next to it. As* NANCY *spies pillow on hall chair, grabs it and comes in,* TOLEN *sits forward and, without looking at him,* NANCY *puts the pillow behind his head. She pulls the chair away from the bed and sits, not facing* TOLEN.)

TOLEN. Why don't you look at me?
NANCY. I can't.
TOLEN. (*Puts down magazine.*) Why can't you?
NANCY. I'll—I'll—
TOLEN. What?
NANCY. I'll laugh.
TOLEN. Why? (*Turns to* NANCY.)
NANCY. You'll make me laugh.
TOLEN. Why? (*Swings legs off bed.*)
NANCY. You will.
TOLEN. Will I?
NANCY. Yes.
TOLEN. Will I? (*Moving in on* NANCY.)
NANCY. Yes.
TOLEN. Look at me, laugh! Go on! Look at me, laugh, look at me, go on, look at me, laugh, look at me, look at me. (TOLEN *is moving right on in, about to kiss* NANCY. *She laughs. She stops laughing. He might kiss her.*)
NANCY. No, no.

COLIN. (*A spasm of nervous, almost pleased, laughter at* TOLEN's *apparent failure.*) Ah HAA!!

(*They both turn to look at* COLIN. *He stumbles* D. L. *in ghastly blushing embarrassment. Pause.*)

TOLEN. You idiot. Fool.

TOM. (TOM *crosses to* NANCY.) Do you like my room?

NANCY. (*Angry and upset without quite understanding what has happened.*) What?

TOM. My room.

NANCY. What! It's not much. There's not much to sit on.

TOM. Sit on the piano. (*Crosses* L., *examining walls.*)

NANCY. (*Irritated.*) Aw!

TOM. They clutter up the place so I really must get them on the wall. (TOM *crosses* C. *looking for right wall to hang chairs on.*)

NANCY. What?

TOM. The chairs. On the wall.

NANCY. What? Oh, it doesn't matter.

TOM. To get them off the floor. (*Crossing to* TOLEN *on bed.*) Have I said anything to upset you, Tolen?

TOLEN. (*Thumbing through "HONEY."*) Nothing you said could possibly upset me. (NANCY *to* U. R. *of window.*) Why do you try and find rational reasons for your childish impulses?

TOM. Do I disturb you?

TOLEN. You make me smile.

TOM. Ooh! He's annoyed. Oh yes, he's annoyed. (*Puts chair down in* U. L. *corner.*) Be careful or you might lose control. (*Climbing up onto ladder.*) Ah well. Back to work. Pass me another cup of tea, Nancy.

NANCY. What?

TOM. Get me another cup of tea, there's a dear.

NANCY. What do you think I am? (NANCY *crosses to* C.)

TOM. Oh. (*Sees that* NANCY *is deeply upset. Pause.*) Sorry.

NANCY. Oh, all right. (*She crosses* D. R. *to tray, pours out tea for* TOM, *crosses back to* TOM, *hands him the cup.*)

TOM. Thanks.

NANCY. (*Crossing* C., *to* TOLEN.) Do you want some?

TOLEN. No. (*Pause.* NANCY *decides to have tea herself. She crosses to tea tray to pour it.* COLIN *crosses to tray, cup extended to have* NANCY *pour him a cup. She never notices* COLIN. *As he reaches the tray, she has finished pouring her own cup. She rises, crosses to suitcases* L. *and sits facing* D. S. *As* COLIN *starts to pour his own tea:*) All right. She's all yours.

COLIN. Eh?

TOLEN. You have a try.

COLIN. (*Puts down teapot as if burned.*) What? Me?

TOLEN. Yes.

(COLIN *takes tea, crosses to* R. *of* NANCY, *who has heard the exchange between* TOLEN *and* COLIN. TOM *is watching the scene from the top of the ladder.* COLIN *is very nervous, turns to* TOM *for help.* TOM *turns* U. S. *as if he'd never seen* COLIN *before.* NANCY *is trying to look unconcerned. Long pause.*)

COLIN. Has Cardiff got big docks?

NANCY. What?

COLIN. Cardiff—the town in Wales—has it got big docks, you know, for ships? (TOLEN *starts to snicker into "HONEY."*)

NANCY. Why ask me?

COLIN. Welsh. I mean—aren't you—don't you come from Wales?

NANCY. No.

COLIN. It was the name—Jones. (TOM *turns to look at* COLIN *in utter amazement.*)

NANCY. Where'd you say the Y.W. was?

COLIN. Oh, it's in Martin's Grove. You have to take a

27 bus, get off at the top of Church Street and walk down on the left until—

NANCY. (*Getting angry.*) It far?

COLIN. Pardon?

NANCY. Is it far?

COLIN. No, not very.

NANCY. Good, I'm going. (*Rises, crosses to* R. *of foot of bed.*)

COLIN. What?

NANCY. I'm off. (*Starting to gather her records and umbrella off bed.*) I said I'm going. As for you, Mr., Mr., Mr. only one name. Mr. no name. (*Shoving* TOLEN'S *feet off her things.*) As for you. As for you. As for you . . . (TOLEN *laughs.* NANCY *spots her magazine in* TOLEN'S *hand, crosses to* U. R. *of bed trying to take it away from him.*) That's my "Honey." Give me my "Honey."

COLIN. (*Crosses* U. C.) I'll take you. I said I'll take you there.

TOLEN. You want your magazine? (TOLEN *grabs her wrist as she tries to get magazine. She tries to pull away but only pulls him after her. They cross* D. R. *to* D. S. *of foot of bed.* TOLEN *kisses her hard and brutally.* NANCY *struggles violently and slowly relaxes to limp.* TOLEN *releases her, leaving her standing limp and yielding. He turns to bed, unconcernedly, picks up "HONEY" and starts to read.*) See? It's not difficult. (NANCY *reacts as if she had been slapped. Bursts into tears, face in hands.* TOM *crosses off ladder,* D. L. *of* TOLEN.)

TOM. Well that's that. I need this room, Tolen.

TOLEN. (*Putting magazine on bed.*) Expecting someone?

TOM. Maybe.

TOLEN. (*Crossing to* D. L. *door.*) Man or woman? (*Stops at door, turns to* TOM.) Are you a homosexual?

TOM. No. (TOLEN *turns, crosses room; when he reaches door:*) Thanks all the same. (TOLEN *exits.*)

(*We hear* TOLEN *running upstairs to his room.*)

COLIN. (*Crossing to* NANCY *to give her the magazine.*) Why do you like annoying him?

TOM. (*Jumps up and down.*) He was annoyed, wasn't he? He's softening up. Ha ha! (*Climbs up on ladder.*) Now he'll play gramophone records and make telephone calls. Really, Colin, what a mess. Suppose the Queen were to come. (*Imitating the Queen's voice.*) "My husband and I are very distressed at the state of this room." Oh this wall, this sickening, everlasting wall, (*Climbs down off ladder looking at unfinished wall.*) it's enormous, it goes on for ever. I'm fed up with it. Here. (*Gives* COLIN *a brush.*)

COLIN. Eh? What's this for?

(TOM *crosses* D. R. *to* NANCY *at window.* TOM *gives* NANCY *a brush.*)

TOM. Only the end bit, the plain bit, the uncreative bit, the bit that don't need genius.

COLIN. You want us to paint the wall?

TOM. The white bit, the boring bit. I'm sick of it.

COLIN. You're so damned lazy.

TOM. (*To* NANCY, *who begins to hit the wall with enthusiasm.*) Attack it. Attack it.

COLIN. And messy. (*Crosses to* D. S. *of* NANCY *to paint under window.*)

NANCY. Yes! Yes! You yes! (*She attacks wall.*) You ha ha! Yes— (*Mumbling between her teeth.*) Yes! Um hm um hm!

TOM. A dear girl. A darling girl. There. That's right. (*Exits through* L. *door.*)

COLIN. Here?

TOM. (*Off.*) Here?

COLIN. The end.

TOM. (*Off.*) The window end?

COLIN. Yes.

TOM. (*Entering with sheet.*) That's right. (*He crosses to window, puts sheet around* NANCY. *He crosses* U. C.

looking at them painting.) Ah yes, that's nice. (TOM *crosses up onto bed, sits on headboard* U. S.) Faster, serfs! (*They start painting faster.*) Elephants! (COLIN *imitates an elephant trumpeting, and then painting with his trunk.*) The Indians keep elephants like we keep cows.—I was wondering how big an elephant's udder was. My God, imagine it swishing around. Do you know, in Walt Disney's early films there were cows and the censor cut the udders out so he put brassieres on them, imagine! . . . Jersey cows wear brassieres, it's true. Jersey cows wear brassieres. (*Beating pillow with umbrella to emphasize his point.*) Something wrong here, cows shouldn't need brassieres. Human beings need them because they stand upright. They used to go on all fours, so they hung downwards—vertically—now they stand upright and it puts on this terrible strain . . . (NANCY *laughs.*) All right, all right. It's true. (TOM *collapses at foot of bed giggling.*)

COLIN. Oh—

TOM. Eh?

COLIN. I wish you wouldn't show off.

TOM. (*To* NANCY.) Hi! (*Rises. To* COLIN.) I don't show off.

COLIN. You do.

TOM. (*Crossing to* NANCY *and moving her* D. S. *away from gray paint which she is in danger of painting white.*) Colin wishes I wouldn't show off. (*Lies down on bed.*)

COLIN. Well, you do show off.

TOM. I don't.

COLIN. You do. (NANCY *has been painting with great vigor.*) Stop slapping it.

NANCY. I like slapping.

COLIN. It's splashing. (*Rises from where he was painting under window.*)

NANCY. So what?

COLIN. It's dripping.

NANCY. I don't care. I don't care.

COLIN. Don't get so excited. (*Crosses* U. S. *of* NANCY.)

NANCY. You're talking. I hear you.
COLIN. Look at her. Look at her. (NANCY *gets carried away and accidentally slaps white paint on grey wall.*)

(*Pause.*)

TOM. Nancy, more left.
NANCY. Oh, sorry. (*She crosses* D. S., *climbs up on window seat to paint up higher.* COLIN *paints same area below her.*) What's the difference between an elephant and a letter box?
COLIN. They can neither of them ride a bicycle.
NANCY. You knew!
COLIN. What? What?
NANCY. I can reach higher than you.
COLIN. Heard it before.
TOM. I don't show off. (*Lying back on bed.*)
COLIN. What? No, you can't.

(*They start jumping up and down trying to reach higher.*)

NANCY. I can.
COLIN. You can't.
TOM. I do—
NANCY. I can—
TOM.—sometimes—
NANCY.—look—
COLIN. You don't—I mean—
NANCY. I can reach higher than you—
COLIN. Ouch!
NANCY. What?
COLIN. It's all run up my elbow. Oh.
TOM. You're dripping everywhere. There's a cloth in the kitchen.

(*Exit* COLIN. *TELEPHONE rings off. Pause. We hear* TOLEN *answer phone Off, then ask the caller to hold on. Enter* TOLEN L., *stands at door.*)

TOLEN. It's for you.

TOM. Man or woman?

TOLEN. Woman. (TOM *rises, crosses* L. *As he passes* TOLEN *snaps his fingers as if to say, "Darn, I hoped it was a man!"* TOLEN *closes the door.* NANCY *turns from her painting, sees she is alone with him at* TOLEN *crosses to her. She jumps off window seat, crosses* U. R., *trying to keep bed between them. He crosses* R. *around bed, she crosses* U. S. *of bed. He crosses* U. S. *of bed, she crosses* L. *to ladder, facing* TOLEN U. S. *of bed.*) No one's going to rape you.

NANCY. Oh!

TOLEN. (*Laughing.*) Girls never get raped unless they want it. (*Steps toward her.*)

NANCY. Oh. (*She backs against ladder, can go no further.*)

TOLEN. I'm sorry about—what happened.

NANCY. That's—

TOLEN. It was clumsy—very—

NANCY. That's all right.

TOLEN. (*Slowly crossing to* NANCY.) It was because they were here—the clumsiness I mean—

NANCY. Was it?

TOLEN. In a way, in a way.

NANCY. Oh.

TOLEN. Don't you believe me?

NANCY. I don't know—I— (*Pulls off sheet, flings it* U. S., *but holds paint brush in front of her to ward him off.*)

TOLEN. (*Crossing to her.*) Please—

NANCY. I—

TOLEN. Please believe me.

NANCY. It doesn't matter.

TOLEN. It does matter, it matters very much. (*Crosses* L. *two steps.*) It matters very much to me. (*Pause.*) How sweet you are. (*He moves to touch her; she thrusts paint brush at him to hold him off. He stops.*) Such a sweet face— (*Moves in.*) such sweetness. (*Touches her face*

tenderly. Pause. He kisses her. As he puts his arms around her, he grabs the paint brush. NANCY *lets go of it and puts her arms around his neck. He is left holding the brush. He tries to edge* NANCY *toward door* D. L.) Ssh . . . ssh . . . Come . . . come up . . . come upstairs . . .
NANCY. Oh . . . oh . . .
TOLEN. Come up to my room.
NANCY. Oh . . . oh . . . no . . .
TOLEN. You like music? I've got some records upstairs . . . I'll play you some records. (*They are still in an embrace.*)

(*CLATTER and BANGING Off.* NANCY *breaks away from* TOLEN *as* COLIN *enters.*)

COLIN. Well, let's get on—oh— (*Realizes he's interrupted something.*) Where are you going? Are you going out? To find the Y.W.? I'll come too.
TOLEN. What? (*Trying to figure out what to do with brush he is still holding.*)
COLIN. I'll come as well.
TOLEN. Where?
COLIN. To find it.
TOLEN. What?
COLIN. The Y.W.

(*Pause.*)

TOLEN. Why don't you go?
COLIN. Eh?
TOLEN. Why don't you go look for the Y.W.?
COLIN. Well, you're coming, aren't you? (TOLEN *is exasperated. He crosses* U. C. *to window, puts brush on window seat, picks up rag there to clean off his hands.*) Well—you—
NANCY. Oh—
COLIN. Oh, come on—
NANCY. I don't think I—
COLIN. Oh, please—

NANCY. What about the cases?
COLIN. The cases?
NANCY. I can't go without them.
COLIN. He'll look after them.
NANCY. Who will?
COLIN. He will.
TOLEN. Me?
NANCY. (*Turns as* TOLEN *moves to go out window.*) Where are you going?
TOLEN. I'm going out. (*Stops.*)
NANCY. (*Crossing to* R. *of* TOLEN.) I'd like a walk.
COLIN. (*Crossing to* L. *of* TOLEN.) So would I.
NANCY. What about the cases?
COLIN. You stay here.
TOLEN. Why should I?
COLIN. You could stay here.
TOLEN. Why should I?
COLIN. You could look after the cases.
TOLEN. He can.
COLIN. Who can?
TOLEN. Tom can.
COLIN. He's upstairs. Can't they stay here? (TOLEN *crosses* D. R. *between bed and* R. *wall.*)
NANCY. I need them at the Y.W.
COLIN. Let's go look for the Y.W. (*Crossing* D. R. *on* L. *side of bed.*)
NANCY. (*Crossing to* TOLEN *at* D. R. *window.*) Are you coming?
TOLEN. To the Y.W.?
COLIN. Well, let's you and me go.
NANCY. Well—
COLIN. Well—
NANCY. I don't think I really—
COLIN. You said you did.
NANCY. Did I?
COLIN. Yes, you did.
NANCY. (*Crossing* U. S. *two steps.*) What about the cases?

ACT II   THE KNACK   57

TOLEN. (*To* COLIN.) Why don't you carry them?
COLIN. Me?
TOLEN. If you're going to the Y.W., why don't you carry them?
COLIN. (*To* NANCY.) Let's go for a walk.
NANCY. What about the cases?
TOLEN. (*To* NANCY.) You carry them.
COLIN. She!
TOLEN. Yes.
COLIN. She can't carry them.
TOLEN. She's already carried them. She carried them here.
COLIN. She can't carry them.
TOLEN. You carry them.
COLIN. I want both hands free.

(*Very angry, very emphatic. Then he blushes as he realizes what he's said. Pause. Enter* TOM D. L. *door.* TOLEN *starts to cross* L.)

NANCY. Where are you going?
TOLEN. (*At door.*) Oh, anywhere. D'you want to?
NANCY. D'you want me to?
TOLEN. If you want to.

(NANCY *runs to* TOLEN.)

COLIN. Are you going to the Y.W.? (*Crossing* L.)
TOLEN. Maybe. (*Exit* TOLEN *and* NANCY.)
COLIN. I'll come too. (*At* D. L. *door.*)
TOLEN. What about the cases? (*Off.*)
COLIN. (*Picks up cases.*) I'll come too.
TOM. (*As* COLIN *goes through door.*) Stay with them, Colin.
COLIN. (*Coming back.*) Eh?
TOM. (*Screams at* COLIN, *waving him to follow them.*) Stick with them.

(*Exit* COLIN. TOLEN *and* NANCY *are seen to pass win-*

dow, followed soon after by COLIN. TOM, *looking very pleased, takes bed to bits and drags it off. Mattress first, then springs, then he wheels off head and foot board as if he were a fat housewife with two children. Just as he reaches* D. L. *door he says in a high falsetto voice,* "Come along, children." *Exits. Re-enters, exhausted. Drinks from the milk bottle on tray. Waters the plant with a little milk. Exits with tray.* TOLEN *and* NANCY *run past window laughing. Door is tried, Off.* TOLEN *and* NANCY *enter through window.*)

TOLEN. That door blocked again? (*Crosses* L. C. *with* NANCY.)

TOM. (*Crossing* R. *to mantel.*) Been moving a few things. (*Enter* COLIN *through window, sits on window seat, as* TOLEN *embraces* NANCY *and they kiss.*) You look very seasick.

COLIN. Shut up. (*He thrusts the shopping bag on his head.*)

(TOM *crosses to* U. S. *chair, moves it* D. R. C. *and sits down, watching* TOLEN *and* NANCY *kissing.*)

TOLEN. We'll go and listen to those gramophone records. (TOLEN *picks up* NANCY. *They are still kissing passionately. They cross to door.* TOLEN *fumbles for the door knob with one hand,* NANCY *clinging to him.* TOLEN *finds knob, exits through door, closes door with his hand still inside room. He struggles to get arm out and shuts the door. Pause. Huge crash off.* TOLEN *re-enters, furious.*) Who put that stuff on the stairs?

TOM. Oh, are the stairs blocked?

TOLEN. I can't get up to my room.

(*Enter* NANCY *giggling.*)

NANCY. Why's the wardrobe on the stairs—and the bed—the stairs are blocked—

ACT II   THE KNACK   59

TOLEN. Stop that! Stop that laughing! Stop it! (*He rushes at* NANCY, *grabs her and slams her against the pillar and throws himself on her as if to rape her.*)

NANCY. Oh! You're hurting me! Let me go! Let me go!

(COLIN *and* TOM *are horrified. They both rush at* TOLEN.)

TOM. Stop. Stop that.

(TOM *and* COLIN *grab* TOLEN *and pull him off. In the struggle,* TOLEN *throws* NANCY *to the floor* R. *Everyone freezes.* TOM R. *of* COLIN, COLIN *at* D. L. *door.* TOLEN L. *of* COLIN *and slightly* D. S. ALL *are focused on* NANCY *lying on the floor* D. L. C. *on a level with* TOLEN. TOM *is the first to move. He crosses* D. S. *to the motionless* NANCY. *He tries to help her up but she jerks away from him.*)

NANCY. Don't touch me! (TOM *retreats* U. L.) Keep off! (*She starts to get to her feet.*) Keep off! D'you hear? Keep away! Don't touch me! You—you—you—don't touch me! (*Crosses* U. C. *to face all THREE of them.* TOM *and* COLIN *react to all of this speech sheepishly.* TOLEN *leans back against the pillar as if he was bored, trying to regain his composure.*) You don't touch me. All right? All right? . . . Now now then, now . . . what's —what's up? What is it, eh? Yes? What you—what you want with me?—What you want— What you trying on, eh? What you trying to do? What is it, eh? What you want—you—you—you . . . Mr. Smart! Mr. Smartie! You think you're— You think you're— You think you're pretty clever. You think you're all right . . . You do, don't you, Mr. Smartie! Mr. Tight Trousers! Mr. Tight Trousers! Mr. Narrow Trousers! You think you're the cat's—you think you're . . . I'll show you . . . I'll show you, Mr. Tight Trousers. Just you don't come near me, d'you hear? Just you don't come near me—come near me, d'you hear? Come near me! I'll show you, Mr. Tight Trousers! Tight Trousers! Yes! Yes! Come near me! Come near me! Come near me! Come! Come! Come! Come! Come!

(TOLEN *laughs.* NANCY *collapses.* COLIN *somehow catches her as she falls.*)

COLIN. She's fainted!
TOM. Lucky there was someone to catch her.

CURTAIN

ACT THREE

Before the CURTAIN rises there is a loud BANGING and CRASHING, mixed with SHOUTS and CRIES. CURTAIN up. COLIN *is holding* NANCY *like a sack of potatoes.* TOM, R. *of bed, and* TOLEN, D. L. *of bed, are putting up the bed against* L. *wall.*

TOM. Give it a bash! And so—oops! A bedmaker, that's you, Tolen, a master bed-wright. (*Picking up mattress and flinging it on bed.*) O.K. Has she come round yet? (*Adjusting mattress.*)

COLIN. Come round?

TOM. Is she still out?

COLIN. Out?

TOM. Oh, he's a thick one. This way.

COLIN. I'm not thick, she's heavy. (COLIN *almost drops her.*)

TOM. Don't drop her. Now we've got this out of the passage, Tolen, you can go upstairs to bed. We'll put her here to rest. Sling her over. (COLIN *slings* NANCY *at* TOM, *knocking* TOM *backwards onto bed with* NANCY'S *limp form on top of him.*) Not like that!

COLIN. You said sling.

TOM. She's in a faint, fainted, can't defend herself.

NANCY. (*Coming to.*) Oh . . . oh dear. . . . (*Crawling around until her face is right over* TOM.) oh dear . . . I do feel . . . I think I'm going to be—

TOM. Sick? (*Slings* NANCY *to one side, leaps off bed, runs for door.* COLIN *runs for bucket,* TOLEN *runs to get out of the way* U. R.) Not here. (COLIN *crosses to* NANCY *on bed, holds out bucket.* TOM *opens door. Crosses back to* NANCY.) Bathroom.

(NANCY *is helped to the door by* TOM, *followed by* COLIN

with bucket. COLIN *crosses to foot of bed, puts bucket under* R. *edge of bed and sits.* TOLEN *closes door after* NANCY *and* TOM *have exited. Locks door.*)

COLIN. What are you doing?
TOLEN. I don't want to be interrupted, Colin. (*Crossing* L. *of bed.*) I have something I wish to discuss with you.
COLIN. Oh, I see . . . But this is Tom's room.
TOLEN. This is your room, Colin, your room. You are the landlord. (*Crossing to* R. *of bed.*) The house belongs to you. It's for you to say whose room this is, Colin. Who lives here.
COLIN. Oh, yes—er—
TOLEN. There is something I would like to discuss with you, Colin. An idea I had.
COLIN. Oh?
TOLEN. You know that you need help, Colin. You do know that, don't you?
COLIN. (*Flopping on bed.*) Mm.
TOLEN. Now tell me, Colin, how many women have you had?
COLIN. Mm . . . (*Sits up slightly.*)
TOLEN. Two women. Only two. And you were late starting, weren't you, Colin? Very late. Not until last year. And Carol left you how many months ago?
COLIN. Mm . . .
TOLEN. Six months ago. (*Crossing* D. R. *to* L. *of ladder.*) That's right, isn't it? Two women in two years. Some of us have more women in two days. I have a suggestion to make to you, Colin. (*Crossing* U. R.) A suggestion which you will find very interesting and which will help you very much. (*Pause.*) Now as you know, Colin, (*Crossing* C.) I have a number of friends. *Men.* And they can help you, Colin, as I can help you. I am thinking particularly of Rory McBride. (*Crosses* L. C.)
COLIN. Oh.
TOLEN. Rory McBride is a man, Colin, a clever man,

a gifted man, a man I can respect. (*Crossing* U. R. *to* COLIN.) He knows a great many things, Colin. Rory McBride was doing things at thirteen that you haven't ever done, Colin! things that you don't even know about.

COLIN. (*Sits right up.*) What sort of things?

TOLEN. In a moment, Colin. (*Crossing* U. R.) First I will tell you my suggestion. Now, as you know, I have a number of regular women, Colin. Women I regularly make. And Rory McBride has a number of regular women too. (*Crossing* C.) Perhaps not quite as many as I have, but several. Now. Quite recently, Rory and I were talking—comparing notes— (*Crossing* D. L.) and we decided it would be a good idea if we saw each other more often . . . (*Crossing* D. L. *to door.*) if even we were to live near each other.

COLIN. (*Turns to* TOLEN.) Oh?

TOLEN. Yes, Colin . . . perhaps in the same house . . . and that we would share our women. (*Crosses* U. L.)

COLIN. Oh!

TOLEN. After I have had a woman, Rory can have her, and if I want I can have Rory's. (*Crosses to* R. *of headboard.*) Of course Rory realizes that it may, in a sense, be dangerous for him. (*Crossing* C.) He may lose a few of his women. However, Rory is well aware that, in the long run, he will profit by the arrangement; he will learn much, Colin, from the women who have been with me.

COLIN. (*Agreeing.*) Mm.

TOLEN. (*Picks up chair, crosses to* COLIN, *sits down, straddling the back of the chair.*) Now, this is the suggestion I have to make. I would consider allowing you to come in on this arrangement.

COLIN. (*Very enthusiastic.*) Oh!

TOLEN. Yes, Colin. I would allow you to come in with Rory and me, share our women. I think you would learn a great deal, Colin.

COLIN. Oh, yes.

TOLEN. It would be a privilege for you, a great privilege.

COLIN. Oh, yes, I see that.

TOLEN. I thought you would appreciate that. I'm sure Rory will agree.

COLIN. Do you think he will?

TOLEN. If I ask him, Colin, he will agree. (*Pause.*) Now, what I suggest, Colin, is that Rory moves into this house.

COLIN. Mm?

TOLEN. In here.

COLIN. Oh . . .

TOLEN. What's the matter, Colin?

COLIN. But there's no room. There's you and me and—

TOLEN. There is this room, Colin. The room you let to Tom. (*Pause.*) Remember this is your room. (*Rises.*) You are the landlord. Rory could have this room and— (*Has crossed R. to replace chair.* TOM *yells off, bangs on door.* COLIN *crosses to door to open it.*) Rory McBride has a Chinese girl, Colin, slinky, very nice, do very well for you. (*This stops* COLIN *just as he is about to unbolt the door.*)

COLIN. (*Turning slowly with lecherous grin on his face.*) Chinese?

TOLEN. (*Crossing D. R. to ladder.*) It's only a question of experience. Of course you'll never be quite so—

(*Through the next speeches* TOM *is heard opening and closing front door.*)

COLIN. Good as— (*Crossing to* TOLEN.)
TOLEN. Me, but—
COLIN. But still—
TOLEN. Oh yes, I don't doubt—
COLIN. You really think—
TOLEN. Certainly!
COLIN. Chinese!

(*Enter* TOM *through* U. S. *window.*)

TOM. What the hell d'you think you're doing? (*Crosses

ACT III THE KNACK 65

D. L.) Why d'you bloody lock the door, Tolen? (*Unlocks door.*) You bloody remember this is my room. (*Crosses U. L. as if looking for something.*)

TOLEN. Oh no, Tom, this is Colin's room.

TOM. Eh? What's going on here? (COLIN *crosses R. of ladder in embarrassment. Small CRASH upstairs.* TOM *yells.*) Stop that! (*Looking about for something.*) Where's her bag? (TOLEN *crosses to mantel, gets bag.*) She wants her bleeding bag. (TOLEN *throws bag to* TOM U. L.) I tell you she's gone bloody funny like a bleeding windmill. (*CRASH Off,* NANCY *yelling.* TOM *exits.*)

TOLEN. (*Crossing C.*) Can you not control your women, Tom? (*To* COLIN.) And a German girl. (*Describes her shape with his hands.*)

COLIN. (*Not quite able to believe his good fortune.*) German!

(TOLEN *crosses to door L., slams it, yanks towel and robe off hook, slings them into corner by door, crosses R. He spars with* COLIN. *As* TOLEN *walks away,* COLIN *follows, imitating his walk.* TOLEN *sees what* COLIN *is doing.* COLIN *turns, sees* TOLEN *is watching him, stops in awkward embarrassment. Throughout the following speech* COLIN *makes a big clockwise circle around chairs.* TOLEN *barks like a drill sergeant.* COLIN *tries desperately and unsuccessfully to walk like* TOLEN. *Each time* TOLEN *gives a new command he believes it will fix the trouble, but it never does,* COLIN *continues to walk ridiculously. By the time* TOM *enters,* COLIN *is marching vigorously around in a grotesque imitation of masculinity.*)

TOLEN. Hold your head up, Colin. Head up! Don't stick your chin out. Move! Move! Move! (TOLEN *crosses U. L. to R. of head of bed as* COLIN *crosses D. R. and starts to circle chairs.*) Keep your belly in. Bend your arms slightly at the elbows—not quite so—that's better. They should swing freely from your shoulders

... Not both together! Keep your head up! Move! Move! Move! Move! Feel it coming from your shoulders, Colin, from your chest! From your gut! From your loin! More loin! More gut, man! Loin! Loin! Move! Move! Move! Move! Keep your head up! Authority, Colin! Feel it rippling through you! Authority! Keep your head up! Authority! Authority!

COLIN. Authority.

TOLEN. Authority! Move! Move! Move! Move! Authority!

TOM. (*Entering.*) You can have a cup of tea ...

(TOLEN *stops, crosses* D. R. *to window seat.* COLIN *continues to walk.*)

NANCY. (*Off.*) Tea!

TOM. Tea.

NANCY. (*In passageway.*) I won't touch it. (*She appears at door* L., *wrapped in blanket.*)

TOM. (*Crosses* C.) For God's sake, make her some tea.

NANCY. I won't touch it. What's that?

TOM. (*Turns to* NANCY.) What's what?

NANCY. That.

TOM. (*Crosses to* NANCY *at bed.* TOLEN *sits on window seat, picks up paper and starts to read it.*) We've lugged this thing in here so you can lie down. Now lie down.

NANCY. I never asked you to bring it in.

TOM. (*Angry.*) You—

NANCY. Don't swear.

(TOM *crosses* D. R., *climbs up on ladder slowly, sits on top.* COLIN *starts to walk around Stage.*)

NANCY. You're not getting me on that thing again, I tell you. Putting that thing together again to tempt a girl. (*Crossing* D. R. *to* TOM.) Hiding it up passages.

Stuffing it here and there. What d'you think I am? Eh? Eh? (*Turns just as* COLIN *passes with his walk.* NANCY *looks in amazement.*) Don't you hear? Can't you hear what I say? (COLIN *is just coming by again.* NANCY *bares her teeth and growls at* COLIN. *He is momentarily disconcerted, stops and crosses* D. L. *in confusion; then ignores her and struts up and down again around chairs.*) An open invitation, if you ask me. Ask me! Go on, ask me! Well, somebody ask me . . . please . . . (*Pause.*) A nasty situation. (*Crosses to* U. S. *of bed.*) Dear me, yes. Very nasty, a particularly vicious sense of— (*Crosses to* L. *of bed.*) criminal, yes, that's it—positively criminal. They ought to be told, somebody should— (*Climbs up on bed.*) I shall phone them, phone them—the police, (*Kneels on bed with blanket around her.*) Scotland Yard, Whitehall one two one two (*She catches sight of* COLIN *walking up and down.*) one two one two (*Repeats "one two" as often as necessary.*)

(COLIN *picks up the rhythm and they begin to work each other up.* NANCY *starts to bang the rhythm.* COLIN *stamps about and slaps himself until eventually he hurts himself.* NANCY *sits on bed temporarily assuaged.* COLIN *goes back to imitating walk* U. R. *around chairs.*)

TOM. That's an interesting movement you've got there, Colin. (*As* COLIN *crosses* D. C.)
COLIN. Oh, d'you think so? (*Crosses to* TOM *on ladder.*)
TOM. Very interesting.
COLIN. Tolen taught it me.
TOM. Oh yes?
COLIN. It's got authority.
TOM. Come again?
COLIN. Authority.
TOM. Ah. Let's see it again . . .

(COLIN *demonstrates, crossing* D. L. TOM *climbs off*

ladder, following him, doing the same exaggerated walk. COLIN *turns at pillar and critically watches* TOM's *imitation.*)

COLIN. You've got to walk from your gut.
TOM. Eh? (*Stops, facing* COLIN.)
COLIN. Your gut.

(TOM *turns to try again.* TOLEN *gets off window seat and stretches.*)

TOM. Oh I see. I see, I see. (TOM *crosses* U. C. *on line, does a very exaggerated masculine sexy walk* D. C. *that gradually turns into a snarling gorilla. At* D. S. *end of cross, he turns and crosses* U. C. *like a German officer, very quiet and sure of his authority.*) Bucket! Bucket!
COLIN. Eh?
TOM. For a helmet. Jump to it! Don't keep me waiting. Bucket!
COLIN. Oh.

(COLIN *jumps for bucket, gives it to* TOM.)

TOM. Now I'll show you what authority's really, Colin. Much more impressive than a shopping bag—a helmet. Dominating, brutal. (*Turns bucket over* COLIN's *head. Crosses* D. R. *to ladder, starts singing "Horst Wessel" and bangs out a 4/4 rhythm.*) Ra ra ra ra, ra ra ra ra, march! March! March! March! Get on with it! Ra ra ra ra. (NANCY *picks up the 4/4 rhythm and the tune.* COLIN *begins to march* L. *to pillar,* R. *to ladder, doing military about-face truns, which turn into goose-stepping gestapo style.*) March! Damn you! March! Jams, guns, guts, butter! Jams, guns, guts, butter! Boots! Boots! Boots! Boots! Boots for crushing! Boots for smashing! Sieg heil! Sieg heil!
COLIN. Sieg heil! Sieg heil!

(*As* COLIN *says the line, he raises his arm in the fascist* salute. *He suddenly realizes what he's doing, stops dead* C. *facing* TOM, R. *Raises the bucket slowly. Their eyes meet.*)

TOM. (*Quietly.*) Ah ha. (TOM *points at* COLIN, *who rips bucket off his head and slings it* U. C.) What's the matter? Don't you like it? I thought you loved it. Tolen loves it, don't you, Tolen? Tolen loves it.

COLIN. Tolen doesn't do that. (*Crosses to* R. *of bed.*)

TOM. Not so loud maybe, but the same general idea. I think it's funnier louder, don't you, Tolen?

COLIN. Shut up. (*Sits on* R. *edge of bed.*)

TOM. Just look at Tolen's boots. (NANCY *crosses to* U. S. L. *corner. To* TOLEN.) Your ears are going red. They're pulsating red and blue. (*Crosses to* TOLEN.) No, I'm exaggerating. One is anyway. The one nearest me. (*Pause.*) That white horse you see in the park could be a zebra synchronized with the railings.

(TOLEN *moves away. Crosses to* TOM, C. *Pause. Crosses* U. C. *to window seat.* TOM *looks very pleased.*)

NANCY. I wouldn't touch it if you made it.
TOM. Eh?
NANCY. I wouldn't.
TOM. Made what?
NANCY. Tea.
TOM. (*To* COLIN.) You'd better make some.
COLIN. (*Disgruntled.*) Oh. (*Crosses* D. L. *as* NANCY *crosses* D. R. *to window.* TOM *crosses to bed and climbs up on it.*)

TOM. Shall I tell you a story? (COLIN *exits* L.) I know you'd like to hear about the kangaroo—the kangaroo. You heard me. Did you? (*Crosses* D. R. *to* NANCY.) Now, of course you know that the baby kangaroo lives in its mother's pouch. Don't you? Go on, commit yourself.

NANCY. Oh, all right. (*Crosses to ladder, climbs up, sits.*)

TOM. Don't be so cautious. This one is true and pure. All my stories are true unless I say so. (*Crosses* R.) Well, the baby kangaroo is born about two inches long and— (*Crossing* L.) as soon as it's born it climbs into its mother's pouch—how does it climb? (*Crosses* R. *to* NANCY.) Never mind, it fights its way through the fur . . . (COLIN *enters balefully and sets down a tray on the bed. Crossing* L.) When it gets inside the pouch the baby kangaroo finds one large, solid nipple. (COLIN *just catches the word as he is about to exit* L. *He catches* TOM's *eye, then exits in confusion.*) Just one. The baby latches on to this nipple and then it, the nipple, swells and swells and swells until it's shaped something like a door knob in the baby's mouth. (*Crossing* R.) And there the baby kangaroo stays for four months, four solid months. What an almighty suck! (TOM *crosses* L. *as* COLIN *enters with teapot and starts to fill the cups on tray.*) Isn't that interesting? Doesn't that interest you as a facet of animal behaviour so affecting human behavior? Doesn't it make you marvel at the vast family of which God made us part? Oh, well . . . (COLIN *crosses* U. C. *to* TOLEN *with tea cup. Pause.*)

NANCY. What happened?

TOM. (*Crosses to* C.) What happened when?

NANCY. You know when.

TOM. (*Crossing to* NANCY *on ladder as* COLIN *crosses to* NANCY *with her tea.*) No, I do not.

NANCY. You know when. (*Seeing cup.*) What's that?

COLIN. (*Between* NANCY *and* TOM, *holding up cup for* NANCY *to take.*) Eh?

TOM. Tea.

NANCY. I'm not having any. I'm not touching it. He's put something in it.

COLIN. Eh?

TOM. Put something in it?

NANCY. Oh, yes, he's put something in it.

TOM. Don't be so daft.

NANCY. I'm not touching it.

Tom. But—
Nancy. I'm not.
Tom. What should he put in it? There's absolutely nothing in it. Nothing at all—look— (*He takes cup, drinks, makes a face as if he were poisoned.*) ugh—! Sugar! (*Staggers* L. *to bed, pours his own cup, crosses to chair* R. *and sits.*)
Nancy. I like sugar.
Colin. (*Handing* Nancy *her cup.*) Two.
Nancy. What?
Colin. Two lumps.
Nancy. (*Taking cup.*) I take two.
Colin. I know.

(Colin *crosses to bed, sets tray on floor. Pours his tea and sits on* R. *edge of bed. A long pause. Rattling of spoons as they all stir their tea. When the last spoon has been put down* Nancy *speaks.*)

Nancy. I've been raped. (*All the* Boys *raise their heads to look at her in unified astonishment.*) I have.
Tolen. I beg your pardon.
Nancy. You heard.
Colin. I didn't.
Nancy. I've been raped.

(Tolen *sneers audibly.*)

Colin. (*Alarmed.*) What!
Nancy. I have been—it was just after—when I fainted —there by the—before I went up with—when I fainted. I was raped.

(Tolen *sneers.*)

Colin. When she says—
Nancy. I have been, you did—
Colin. Does she mean really—I mean, actually?

TOM. What else?
NANCY. Rape. Rape. I—I've been—
COLIN. But—
NANCY. Raped.
COLIN. But you haven't.
NANCY. I have.
COLIN. No one has—
NANCY. Rape.
COLIN. But we've been here all the time, all of us.
NANCY. Huh!
COLIN. You know we have.
TOLEN. A vivid imagination, (*Crossing* D. C. *on a level with* TOM.) that's what's the matter with her.
NANCY. Eh?
COLIN. Oh?
TOM. Watch it.
TOLEN. Take no notice of her.
NANCY. Eh?
TOLEN. Ignore her. (*Crossing* C.)
NANCY. What? Rape?
TOM. You be careful, Tolen.
NANCY. Rape! I been—
TOLEN. She quite simply wishes to draw attention to herself.
NANCY. (*A little unsure.*) Oh?
TOLEN. She has fabricated a fantasy that we have raped her. First because she wants us to take notice of her and second because she really would like to be raped.
NANCY. Eh?
COLIN. Would you mind saying that again?
TOLEN. (*Crossing to* COLIN.) Her saying that we have raped her is a fantasy. She has fabricated this fantasy because she really does want to be raped; (NANCY *crosses off ladder and* U. C. *to* R. *of* TOLEN.) she wants to be the center of attention. The two aims are, in a sense, identical. The fabrication that we have raped her satisfactorily serves both purposes.
COLIN. Oh.

NANCY. (*Crossing to* TOM, C.) What's that word mean? Fabricated?

TOLEN. Made it up.

NANCY. (*A bit nonplussed, she crosses back to* R. *of* TOLEN.) Oh no. Oh no. Not that. I'm not a fool you know—I'm not a ninny . . . (TOLEN *sits on bed* U. S. *of* COLIN.) No, no, I didn't make it up . . . (*Crosses* C.)

TOM. (*To* TOLEN.) What'll you do if she tells everyone you raped her?

TOLEN. What?

TOM. There's a methodist minister lives two doors down. Suppose she was to yell out of the window?

TOLEN. Are you mad?

TOM. (*To* NANCY.) Don't let him off so easily, love.

NANCY. Eh?

TOM. (*To* TOLEN.) What'll you do if she yells down the street?

NANCY. Rape! (*Runs to* U. S. *window, sticks her head out yelling like one possessed.*) They done me! Rape! You done me! You did! Rape! Rape! Rape! Rape! (*Repeats as often as necessary.*)

(*Meanwhile,* TOLEN *and* COLIN *run* U. C., TOLEN *grabs* NANCY *and pulls her back inside.*)

TOLEN. Shut the window.

(*As* COLIN *shuts the window tight,* NANCY *skips* D. C. *and starts to skip to far* D. S., *saying "Rape, rape" in a sing-song.*)

NANCY. You don't want me yelling down the street, do you?

(COLIN *crosses to* U. S. *of bed.*)

TOLEN. We don't want the trivial inconvenience.

NANCY. (*Skipping.*) You're scared they'll hear and lock you up.

TOLEN. (*Crossing D. R. to pose like Napoleon L. of ladder.*) I do not intend to expose myself to trivial indignities from petty officials.

NANCY. (*Crossing D. L. and climbing up onto bed.*) You're worried. You're scared. You're afraid. I'll tell. I will tell!

COLIN. Eh?

NANCY. (*Jumping up and down on bed shouting in triumph at* TOLEN.) The police. The Y.W. I'll report you. That's it. (COLIN *grabs the head of the bed, afraid it will collapse under her.*) The lot. Them all. I'll tell them how you raped me—how you— I'll tell them. The coppers. The Y.W.

TOM. (*Enjoying it all.*) Whew!

NANCY. (*Leaping up and down in glee at their discomfort.*) All the lurid details! All the horrid facts! *News of the World.* T.V. Read all about it! Rape! Rape! Just you wait! You'll get ten years for this!

TOM. She means it. (*Rises to his feet.* NANCY *stands on the bed watching the following scene.*)

TOLEN. She's simply drawing attention to herself.

COLIN. Means what?

TOM. She means to tell everyone we raped her. (*Collapses into chair.*) Right. (*Putting* TOLEN *on the spot.*) In that case he must rape her.

COLIN. Eh?

TOLEN. I beg your pardon?

TOM. In that case she must be raped by him.

NANCY. I'm not having it twice.

TOM. You want her to keep quiet.

TOLEN. I do not propose to allow her to expose . . .

TOM. (*Cutting him short.*) Right. You say she's made this up because she really does want to be raped.

COLIN. Well?

TOM. If he wants to keep her quiet he must rape her.

According to what he says—and he's probably right—that's the only thing will satisfy her.

COLIN. (*To* TOM.) If she's raped she'll be the center of attention, that's it!

TOM. Just so. What do you say?

(*The men are talking about* NANCY *but, in a sense, have forgotten her. She is resentful.*)

NANCY. Rape!

TOM. What do you say, Tolen?

(*Pause.*)

TOLEN. It's your idea. Why don't you rape her?

TOM. I like her yelling down the street.

(*Pause.*)

TOLEN. Colin?

COLIN. What, me?

NANCY. Rape!

COLIN. Oh no. I couldn't. (*He crosses to* TOLEN. TOM *turns to look at* TOLEN *and* COLIN.)

(*Pause.*)

TOLEN. I never yet came to a woman under duress and certainly never because I was forced to it. (NANCY *slips off bed and crosses* U. C. *to window.*) Because she demanded it. (NANCY *unlatches window.*) Because I had to buy her silence. (NANCY *sticks her head out of window.*) I shall not now. (NANCY *yells.*)

NANCY. Rape! (*She continues yelling as long as is necessary.*)

COLIN. Stop her! (*Crosses to grab her.*)

TOLEN. Don't let her— (*Crosses to* NANCY.)

TOM. Whoops! Whoops!

(TOLEN *grabs for* NANCY *but only gets the blanket.* NANCY *runs* D. L. COLIN *starts after her.* TOLEN *grabs him to make him shut the window while he goes after* NANCY. NANCY *hides behind the open door* L. TOLEN *exits* L.; *as* NANCY *closes it behind him,* COLIN *shuts the window.* NANCY *runs* R., *behind ladder, yelling "Rape!"* TOM *cuts her off between ladder and chair.* COLIN *cuts her off between ladder and wall. She is trapped, giggling, loving it.* TOLEN *re-enters* L., *blanket still in his hand, and crosses to group at ladder shouting, "I'll get ther! I'll get her!"* TOM *goes to grab* NANCY *at the same moment that* TOLEN *throws blanket in attempt to ensnare* NANCY *and gets* TOM *instead.* NANCY *dashes out* L.)

TOLEN. Shut the door! Shut the door! (COLIN *rushes to door, slams it shut and bolts it.* NANCY'S *footsteps are heard running upstairs.* COLIN *throws himself across the door.* TOLEN *crosses to* COLIN *in a rage at his stupidity.*) The front. The front door. She'll get out the front. Colin!

(COLIN *exits through* U. S. *window. BANGING Offstage at front door.* TOLEN *exits into passage at same time.* TOM *crosses to chair, sits, drinks his tea. Re-enter* COLIN *and* TOLEN.)

COLIN. No, she won't. It's blocked.

(NANCY *is heard coming downstairs. Then a SOUND of something being smashed.*)

TOM. She smashed up the bathroom. I wonder what that was.
TOLEN. My records!

(TOLEN *runs to door. Enter* NANCY, *wearing only her slip. In her hands she carries her shoes, hose, garter belt, dress and raincoat. She skips around the room flinging the clothes all over it.* TOM *chases her, trying to stop her,* COLIN *tries to clear the tea things so they won't get smashed.* TOLEN *remains* D. L. *by door.*)

NANCY. (*Skipping.*) Shove you in jug! Put you in jail! One for the road! Long for a stretch! Just you wait! I'll tell! (*As* TOM *chases* NANCY *he is frantically gathering up her clothes as she flings them away; he pleads her to stop.*) I shall sue you for paternity.
TOM. Now listen, Nancy.
NANCY. All of you.
TOM. Nancy.
NANCY. Don't Nancy me.
TOM. (NANCY *ad-libs through this speech.*) Look, love—don't say anything for a minute. Now look, we haven't raped you—but—just a moment— Now listen, everything's happening so fast you must give us a chance to think. (TOM *finally corners* NANCY U. R. *corner just as* COLIN *gets the last teacup to safety in the same corner.*) I mean you're a reasonable girl, Nancy, an intelligent girl, gives us a chance now, just give us a chance like a reasonable, intelligent girl, just let us talk for one moment. No yelling and no dashing off anywhere. (TOM *pushes the pile of her clothes into her hands in desperation.*)
NANCY. It's a trap.
TOM. No it isn't. I promise. It's pax for one minute.
NANCY. All right. I'll give you one minute.
TOM. That's not enough.
NANCY. Two minutes.
TOM. Five.
NANCY. Three.
TOM. Done. (*Followed by* COLIN, *he crosses* D. L. NANCY *crosses* D. C.)
NANCY. Three minutes and no more. Then I'll start yelling again. (*She throws all of the clothes into the air, and they come raining down all over.*) Lend me a wrist watch.

TOM. Oh, very well. Colin! (COLIN *stops and gives her his wrist watch; starts to cross* D. L.)

NANCY. And if you're naughty and cheat I can smash it.

COLIN. (*Turning back to* NANCY.) Oh, I say—

TOM. Oh come on, Colin.

(NANCY *climbs the stepladder, sits on top of it, facing out.* AUTHOR'S NOTE: *the following scene falls into four sections.*)

(*1ST SECTION: Introduction to the scene: The* THREE *confer.* TOLEN *is* R. *of pillar,* COLIN *is* L. *of pillar,* TOM *is seated on little* D. S. *table.*)

TOM. Now, Tolen.

TOLEN. The situation is quite clear.

COLIN. Not to me it isn't.

TOM. You've got to rape her.

TOLEN. Please be quiet, Tom.

TOM. Oh, go on.

TOLEN. An impasse has been reached.

COLIN. She believes we've raped her.

TOM. She's convinced herself.

TOLEN. She's made it up to draw attention to herself and because she wants it.

TOM. She is prepared to report us.

COLIN. Yes, yes.

TOM. Tolen doesn't want that.

COLIN. No, no.

TOM. But he's not prepared to do the other thing.

COLIN. What are we going to do?

NANCY. (*While the* OTHERS *confer.*)
I've been raped, I've been raped
I've been raped, raped, raped,
I've been raped, I've been raped,
I've been raped, raped, raped,
I've been raped, I've been raped—

(TOLEN *breaks away when* NANCY *starts up. The other* TWO *turn and watch* TOLEN *as he crosses to* NANCY. *He stands with hands on hips glaring at her,* L. *of ladder.* NANCY *falls silent.* TOLEN *turns, crosses back* L., NANCY *makes faces at his back.*)

TOLEN. She must be examined by a competent physician.
COLIN. What?
TOLEN. A doctor. If she's a virgin—that lets us out.
COLIN. What if she's not?

(*Pause.*)

TOM. If she's not a virgin she could say we raped her and we'd have a job to prove otherwise.
TOLEN. She must be a virgin.
TOM. Why should she be?
TOLEN. Well, take a look at her.

(*They* ALL *look at her.*)

NANCY. Two minutes gone. One minute to go.
TOLEN. Obviously a virgin.
TOM. I don't see why, it doesn't necessarily follow.
COLIN. Follow what?
NANCY. Finished?
TOM. No.
NANCY. Ninety seconds to go.
COLIN. Mind the watch.
NANCY. Rape!
TOLEN. Don't get so excited, Colin.
COLIN. It's my watch.

(*2ND SECTION:* TOM *begins to enjoy the humor of the situation, and states his attitude; so that* TOLEN *also states* his *attitude.*)

TOM. Since you take this attitude, there seems no rational course other than to negotiate. Open negotiation.

TOLEN. Negotiate!

TOM. Negotiate. (*Crosses* S. R. *of pillar as if going to* NANCY.)

TOLEN. Negotiate with a woman. Never. (*Crosses to* L. *of pillar.*)

TOM. Then what is your suggestion? (*Crosses to* R. *of pillar.*)

TOLEN. Authority.

COLIN. Oh?

TOLEN. Authority.

COLIN. Ah!

TOLEN. In all his dealings with women a man must act with promptness and authority—even, if need be, force.

COLIN. Force?

TOM. Force?

TOLEN. Force.

(*3RD SECTION:* COLIN *decides that* TOLEN'S *attitude is correct.*)

TOM. I cannot agree to force and certainly not to brutality.

TOLEN. Never negotiate.

TOM. Calm, calmth.

NANCY. Sixty seconds.

TOLEN. Force.

TOM. Negotiate. Parley, parley.

TOLEN. Negotiate with a woman—

TOM. Calm.

TOLEN. Never! Force!

COLIN. He's—

TOLEN. Force. Force.

COLIN. For—

TOM. Calm, calm, calmth.

TOLEN. Force, force. Never negotiate.

COLIN. For—for—

TOM. No brutality!

ACT III THE KNACK 81

COLIN. Force!
TOLEN. Never negotiate! Eh?
COLIN. Force! Force!
TOM. Oh!
COLIN. Force! Force! In dealing with a w-w-w-w-
NANCY. Forty seconds to go!
COLIN. —w-woman a man must act with promptness and authority.
TOLEN. Force.
COLIN. Force.

(TOLEN *shoves* COLIN R., *delighted with him.* TOM *is* D. L. *of* COLIN, R., *and* TOLEN L.)

(*4TH SECTION:* COLIN *is precipitated into a forceful course of action.*)

TOM. Parley, negotiate.
TOLEN. Authority.
TOM. Parley.
TOLEN. Force.
COLIN. Force.
TOM. No, no, parley, parley!
COLIN. Force.
TOLEN. Force.
NANCY. Twenty.
TOM. Parley, parley.
TOLEN. No, no. Force.
COLIN. For! For! For! He's right!
NANCY. Ten seconds to go.
COLIN. Force.

(*The following should tumble across each other as the excitement mounts.*)

TOLEN. Force.
TOM. Parley.
NANCY. Eight.

COLIN. Force.
TOLEN. Never negotiate.
TOM. Calm.
COLIN. He's right, he's absolutely right!
TOLEN. Force.
NANCY. Four.
COLIN. A man—
NANCY. Three.
COLIN. Must—
NANCY. Two.
COLIN. Use—
NANCY. One.
COLIN. Force. (TOLEN *shoves* COLIN C.) Shut up! Just you shut your—d'you hear! You're talking through your— Firmness! (*To* TOLEN *and* TOM *for confirmation.*) A firm hand! Spanking! See who's— (*Crossing to* NANCY.) I've been here all the time, d'you hear? All the time. You've not been raped. (TOM *crosses to bed and flops, sprawling in exhaustion.*) You have not. I know. So stop squawking. I know. I've been here all the time. (*Crosses to* L.)

NANCY. Ah.

COLIN. (*Crossing to* NANCY.) I've been here all the time. So I can prove, prove, testify, I have seen nothing. You've not been raped. I know. I've been here all the time.

NANCY. Ah.

COLIN. (*Crossing* U. C., *indicating her heap of clothes.*) Come on down now and get them on. Get your clothes on. Come down, come down, you silly little . . . (*Crossing to* L. *of* NANCY.) little messer. You've not been raped, I know. I've been here all the time.

NANCY. You!

COLIN. (*Turning* L. *to show off to* TOLEN.) I've been here all the time!

NANCY. You did it! It was you!

COLIN. I been here . . . (*Jerks around to face* NANCY.) Eh?

NANCY. You! You! You! He did it! He raped me! He's been here all the time! He says so! He has! Yes, he raped me!

COLIN. Me!

NANCY. You.

TOM. Him! (*Rises, pointing at* COLIN.)

COLIN. Me!

NANCY. Yes, you. You been here all the time.

TOM. You, she says. She says you did it. (*Sinks to bed.*)

COLIN. Me.

NANCY. Yes. You'll get ten years.

COLIN. Me, me? Me! Oh, no. This is awful. You're making a terrible mistake.

NANCY. Oh no, not likely. I've been here all the time.

COLIN. Oh, oh you are—tell her, someone. Someone, (*Running* L. *to* TOLEN *and* TOM *for help.*) Tolen, tell— her I didn't. No really, I mean—

NANCY. I got a head on my shoulders.

COLIN. I can see that but— (*Turns back to* NANCY.)

NANCY. That's it, you. You raped me.

COLIN. But—but I assure you— I mean— (*Crossing* D. C.)

NANCY. That's him, officer, that's the one.

COLIN. No! Tolen—Tom—please. (*Crossing* U. L. *to* TOM. *in a desperate state.*) I mean I didn't, really I didn't.

NANCY. Clothes!

COLIN. Clothes? (*Turns to* NANCY.)

NANCY. Tore them off me.

COLIN. Tore them—oh no. (*Crossing to* NANCY.)

NANCY. Scattered.

COLIN. No. (*Backing* U. C.)

NANCY. There they are.

TOM. Clear evidence.

NANCY. (*Crossing off ladder to* COLIN.) That face. You'd never know, they'd never guess.

COLIN. Oh, wouldn't they? (*Backing* U. C.)

NANCY. No girl would ever suspect.
COLIN. Oh?
NANCY. But underneath—
COLIN. What?
NANCY. Raving with lust.
COLIN. Oh no, I mean— (*Crossing* D. R. *to ladder.*)
NANCY. Fangs dripping with blood. (*Crossing* U. L.)
COLIN. Oh.
NANCY. (*Whirls on* COLIN *from* R. *of bed.*) Bones of countless victims hidden in the basement. (*Crosses to* C.)

COLIN. We haven't got a basement. No! No! I mean I didn't, really I didn't. I didn't rape you— I mean I wouldn't—but well—this is terrible! Me! . . . You really think I did?

NANCY. Of course.

COLIN. I mean you really do think I did?

NANCY. Yes.

COLIN. You really do! (*Turns away, suddenly very happy to think that a woman thinks he has enough virility to rape someone.*)

NANCY. Wait till next Sunday. What's your job?

COLIN. Eh? I'm a school teacher. (*Turning to* NANCY.)

NANCY. School teacher rapes Nancy Jones!

COLIN. Oh!

NANCY. Little did the pupils at—at—

COLIN. Tottenham Secondary Modern—

NANCY. Tottenham Secondary Modern realize that beneath the handsome exterior of their tall, fair-haired blue-eyed school teacher there lurked the heart of a beast— (*Crossing* D. *to* COLIN.) lusting for the blood of innocent virgins—little did they— (*Crossing* U. C.) You wait till you see the "Sunday Pictorial." (*Turns back to* COLIN.)

COLIN. Oh, I say, me. Me. Me. Oh I say. Oh. Oh. Do you really think—?

NANCY. What?

COLIN. I've got a handsome exterior?

ACT III   THE KNACK   85

NANCY. Well—rugged perhaps, rather than handsome. (*Looking him over.*) And strong.

COLIN. Oh.

NANCY. Oh yes, ever so. And lovely hands.

COLIN. Oh, oh, oh . . . Are you—are you doing anything tonight? (*Crossing toward* NANCY.)

NANCY. What? (*Backing up.*)

COLIN. Are you doing anything tonight? (*Crossing toward her.*)

NANCY. Oh! (*Backing into bed.*)

COLIN. Oh, please, I didn't mean that. I mean I didn't rape you, anyway, I mean, oh well. Look, I mean let's go to the pictures or something or a walk or a drink or anything, please. I think you're simply—I mean— Oh golly—do you really think I did? I mean I didn't rape you but I would like to.

NANCY. What!

COLIN. I mean—I would like to take you to the pictures or something.

NANCY. (*Crossing* D. R.) Well, I don't know, it doesn't seem quite right somehow . . .

COLIN. Oh please—

NANCY. Well— (*Stops at ladder.*)

COLIN. The pictures or anything. (*Crossing to* NANCY.)

NANCY. (*Turning back to* COLIN.) Would you?

COLIN. Oh, yes, I would.

TOLEN. (*Still* D. L., *watching the whole scene.*) This I find all very amusing.

TOM. I thought you might.

TOLEN. Hilarious.

TOM. I've always admired your sense of humor.

COLIN. Eh?

TOM. (*Rises up on bed, very pleased.*) Well done. Very good. You're getting on very nicely, Colin. Much better than the great Tolen.

TOLEN. That sexual incompetent.

COLIN. Eh?

NANCY. He's not incompetent. (*She crosses* C.) What's incompetent? (*Crossing* U. L. *to* TOM.)

TOM. No good.

NANCY. No good? (*Crosses* D. L. *to* TOLEN.) He's marvelous. He raped me.

TOLEN. You have not been raped.

NANCY. I have. (*Crossing to* TOLEN, *right to his face.*)

(*During the following,* TOM *rises, crosses to ladder* D. R., *picks up ladder, carries it* U. L. *to* U. S. *wall,* L. *of window. Takes nails and hammer out of box, climbs ladder and starts driving nails into wall about nine feet above floor level. His banging deliberately punctuates the following dialogue.*)

TOLEN. You have not been raped and you know it.

NANCY. He raped me.

TOLEN. You have not.

NANCY. I have.

TOLEN. And certainly not by—

NANCY. Rape.

TOLEN. Him. He wouldn't know one end of a woman from the other.

NANCY. Rape, rape.

TOLEN. The number of times I've seen him. "Has Cardiff got big docks?" He'll never make it, never.

COLIN. What? (*Crosses to* R. *of* NANCY.)

TOLEN. Granted—

COLIN. What did you say?

NANCY. He raped me.

TOLEN. Granted he might do better with help—and he needs help. Bow-legged, spavin-jointed, broken-winded, down and out. Look at him.

COLIN. Eh?

NANCY. (*Turning back to* COLIN.) He's rugged.

TOLEN. I ask you is it possible—?

NANCY. Handsome.

TOLEN. Or likely—?

NANCY. Marvellous, super.
TOLEN. It takes him four months hard labor to get a girl to bed.
NANCY. He did, you did, didn't you?
TOLEN. That oaf.
NANCY. Go on, tell him.
COLIN. What was that bit about hard labor?
TOLEN. You keep out of this.
NANCY. (*Patting* COLIN *on head.*) Yes, you shut up.
TOLEN. A rapist, oh really.
NANCY. (*Turns back to* TOLEN, *taunting him.*) Rape, rape.
TOLEN. That chicken.
NANCY. Rape.
TOLEN. How stupid can you get? Too ridiculous.
NANCY. Rape. Rape. (NANCY *skips about* U. S. *and continues around the room, ad-libbing "Rape" through rest of this.* NANCY's *indignation is transformed into delight.* TOM *is pleased at the way things are developing. They should form a light-hearted counterpoint to the dialogue between* COLIN *and* TOLEN. *The scene should be gay, musical, quite free from strain and shouting.*)
TOLEN. Probably impotent.
COLIN. (*Crosses right in to* TOLEN.) Why not?
TOLEN. What?
COLIN. Why not me, pray?
NANCY. Rape. Rape.
COLIN. Why not me? (*To* TOM.) Be quiet. (*To* TOLEN.) Sexually incompetent! Hard labor!
NANCY. Rape pape pape pape pape pape—

(TOM *continues banging.*)

COLIN. (*To* TOM.) Shut up. (*To* TOLEN.) Now, you listen—
TOM. Rape!
NANCY. R e e e e e ep.
COLIN. All, all I can say is outrage. Outrage. Outrage.

(*To* Tom.) Shut up. (*To* Tolen.) Rape, rape, didn't I? Couldn't I? I did— (*To* Tom.) Shut up. (*To* Tolen.) Now, you listen, now get this straight— (*To* Tom.) Shut up. (*To* Tolen.) I am not incapable!

Nancy. Rape! Reep! Raaaaaape!

Colin. (*Turning* u. s. *to* Tom.) Shut up. Shut up.

(Nancy *is now keeping up an almost permanent chirrup.* Tom *is finished with hammering. He crosses* d. r. *and sits on window seat waiting.* Tolen *crosses* u. s. *of window.*)

Colin. Shut up, shut up. (*Turns back to* Tolen, *who has moved.* Colin *finds him,* r., *crosses to him.*) Now get this, get this—get—get—shut up—I could've I'd wanted—rape her—shut up—I didn't—you think I couldn't—shut up—I—I—shut! Shut! I'll show you! (Colin *starts to chase* Nancy *round the bed.* Nancy *is at* u. s. *end of bed between* l. *wall and bed.* Colin *goes to foot of bed to get behind the bed.* Nancy *runs* r. *shoving bed.* Colin *chases her around the bed.*) Just let me —get her—I'll—I'll show you—I'll—I'll—yes I'll—just you I'll show—oh—oh—oh—oh—oh—

Nancy. Oh—oh—oh—oh—

Colin. Oh—oh—oh—oh—

Nancy. Oh—oh—oh—oh—

(Colin *at head of bed,* r., Nancy *at foot,* l., *trying to feint each other.*)

Tolen. You can't even catch her, Colin, can you? Never mind rape her. I think you are quite incapable of making a woman, Colin. (Colin *breaks for* Nancy. Nancy *keeps bed between them, runs to head.*) Look, I'll show you. (Tolen *grabs* Nancy *and pulls her close as* Colin *crosses* r., *shoves bed violently into wall* l.)

Colin. If you touch her—I'll kill you!

(*Very long pause.* Tolen *releases* Nancy *who goes to* Colin. *A* Girl *passes the window.* Tolen *laughs gently and then exits through* U. S. *window.* NANCY *crosses* D. L. TOM *crosses* U. L., *hoists chairs onto the nails in the wall.* COLIN *is gathering* NANCY'S *things.*)

TOM. (*Crosses* D. R. *to window, turns* U. S. *to survey his work.*) Ah yes, beautiful. (*He crosses* D. L., *pauses to look with approval at* COLIN *and* NANCY. *As he exits* S. L. *door.*) Ah, yes.

(COLIN *pulls the bed* C., NANCY *follows.* COLIN *at head,* NANCY *at foot.* COLIN *puts all her things in the center of the bed.* NANCY *puts* COLIN'S *watch on the bed.* COLIN *handbalances on headboard and shyly looks at* NANCY *for the first time since* TOLEN'S *exit, with a big grin on his face.* NANCY *smiles at him, peeking over the footboard.*)

CURTAIN

COSTUMES AND PERSONAL PROPS

NANCY:

Raincoat—(blue slicker)
Dress—(yellow—break-a-way back zipper)
Slip—(full length white)
Shoes—(brown)
Shoulder bag—(brown)
Hand mirror—(in bag)
Half slip
Petti pants
Slip of paper (YWCA Martin's Grove W2) (in coat pocket)

TOM:

Sweatshirt—(white) ⎫
Dungarees   ⎬ paint spattered
Sneakers—(white)   ⎪
Socks—(black)   ⎭

COLIN:

Shirt—(blue)
Slacks—(grey wool)
Socks—(black)
Shoes—(brown)
Wristwatch—(expansion band)

TOLEN:

T-shirt—(short sleeve—black)
Slacks—(black)
Jacket—(black—windbreaker)
Socks—(black)
Boots—(black)
Gloves—(black leather)
Belt—(brown)
Sunglasses—(black wrap-a-round)
"Little Black Book"
Nail file

FURNITURE AND PROPERTY LIST

ACT I

On Stage:
English newspaper
Rags
Empty (2 gal.) can
Plant (live)
7 brushes
> *One each:*
> 1" black
> 2" black
> 3" grey
> 3" (spare)
> 4" (dry)
> 4" white
> 6" white

White paint (2 gal. can)
Black paint (1 gal. can)
Grey paint (1 gal. can)
Large plastic bucket
Chest expanders
5' step ladder
Paint can (empty 1 gal.)
2 chairs
4 trees
Mattress
Divan
Milk crate
Hammer
2—6" nails
Wardrobe
2 chairs (arm)
Dresser
Robe
Bath towel
Small table
Dresser (small)
Clock
Shoe boxes
2 lampshades
Picture
Suit jacket

FURNITURE AND PROPERTY LIST

Off Stage:
  Windolene bottle and rag
  Large suitcase
  Small suitcase
  Shopping bag with:
    2 records
    Honey magazine
    Umbrella
  Bed—head, foot, spring
  Box of raisins

ACT II

On Stage:
  SAME PLUS:
  Bed—head, foot, spring, mattress
  Shopping bag
  Honey magazine
  2 records
  Umbrella

Off Stage:
  Road map of London
  Tea tray with:
    4 cups
    4 spoons
    English milk bottle with milk
    Tea pot with tea
    Plate of biscuits
    Bowl of sugar cubes
  Pillow
  Sheet

Strike:
  Divan
  Raisins
  Windolene

ACT III

On Stage:
  SAME

Off Stage:
  Tea tray with:
    4 cups

FURNITURE AND PROPERTY LIST

4 spoons
Milk bottle
Bowl of sugar cubes
Tea pot
"Navy" blanket
Prop raincoat
Prop dress
Garter belt
Stockings

Strike:
Sheet
Pillow
Tea tray and tea things

Supplies:
Wallpaper
Glue
Wallpaper brush
White paint
Black paint
Brown tint
Shopping bags
"Social tea" biscuits
Milk
Sugar cubes
Chemprox
Coke bottles
DOUBLES ON ALL COSTUMES AND PROPS

Off Stage "Props":
Crash box
Bed spring
3 iron pipes
Toilet plungers
Tapes—Music
Motorbike
Phone
Crash door

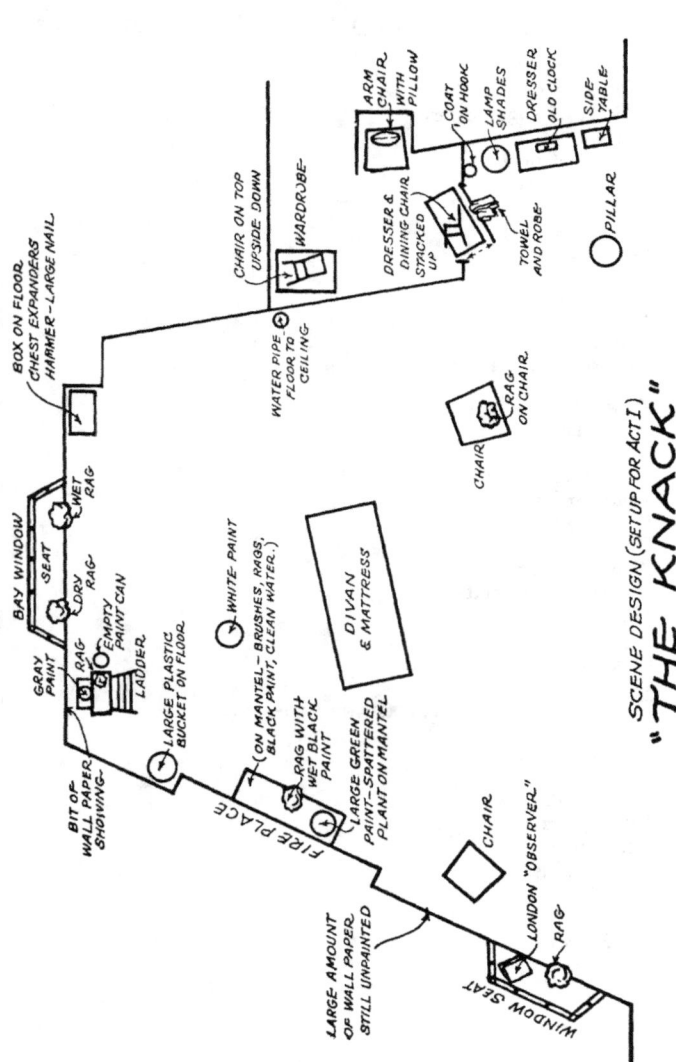

MUSIC USE NOTE

Licensees are solely responsible for obtaining formal written permission from copyright owners to use copyrighted music in the performance of this play and are strongly cautioned to do so. If no such permission is obtained by the licensee, then the licensee must use only original music that the licensee owns and controls. Licensees are solely responsible and liable for all music clearances and shall indemnify the copyright owners of the play(s) and their licensing agent, Samuel French, against any costs, expenses, losses and liabilities arising from the use of music by licensees. Please contact the appropriate music licensing authority in your territory for the rights to any incidental music.

IMPORTANT BILLING AND CREDIT REQUIREMENTS

If you have obtained performance rights to this title, please refer to your licensing agreement for important billing and credit requirements.

www.ingramcontent.com/pod-product-compliance
Lightning Source LLC
Chambersburg PA
CBHW051408290426
44108CB00015B/2196